# Journey to the Esoteric Circle

## Reclaiming your Cosmic Birthright during the Apocalypse

by Peter Denbo Haskins

That's great, it starts with an earthquake
Birds and snakes, and aeroplanes
And Lenny Bruce is not afraid
Eye of a hurricane, listen to yourself churn
World serves its own needs
Don't mis-serve your own needs
Speed it up a notch, speed, grunt, no, strength
The ladder starts to clatter
With a fear of height, down, height
Wire in a fire, represent the seven games
And a government for hire and a combat site
Left her, wasn't coming in a hurry
With the Furies breathing down your neck
Team by team, reporters baffled, trumped, tethered, cropped
Look at that low plane, fine, then
Uh oh, overflow, population, common group
But it'll do, save yourself, serve yourself
World serves its own needs, listen to your heart bleed
Tell me with the Rapture and the reverent in the right, right
You vitriolic, patriotic, slam fight, bright light
Feeling pretty psyched

It's the end of the world as we know it and I feel fine.

**-It's the end of the world as we know it (and I feel fine) by R.E.M. from 'Document' 1987**

# Table of Contents

Introduction                    7

Chapter One                    15

Chapter Two                    33

Chapter Three                  49

Chapter Four                   65

Chapter Five                   79

Chapter Six                    89

Chapter Seven                 105

Chapter Eight                 125

Chapter Nine                  173

Epilogue                      223

# Introduction:
## Welcome to the Journey

The word: 'Apocalypse'. What is your first thought when you hear that word? What fantastic and frightening images this word conjures up, right? It's used so much in our Western vocabulary that it has nearly lost any connection to its original meaning. Our present-day usage of the word for a 'cataclysmic event' began in the 1850's but if we dive deeper into its roots, we see that in Middle English it was used to describe an 'insight, vision or hallucination.' It's original meaning however comes from the Greek (*apokalyptein*) to 'uncover, disclose or reveal.' It was translated as 'revelation' by John Wycliffe in his 14th Century English translation of the Holy Bible and has become the most fantastically creative and frustratingly elusive final book within Christianity's Holy Scripture. In its root meaning 'kel' (Proto-Indo-European) 'to cover, conceal, save,' we see that this root meaning can be applied to words such as 'helmet' or a 'hold' as in the space in a ship below the lower deck or a 'hull' as in the covering of a seed.' In the Sanskrit of this root word, the meaning alludes to 'hut, house, hall,' in the Middle Irish 'cul' alludes to 'defense or shelter' and in the Old Prussian 'au-klipts' it alludes to something that is 'hidden.' (from *etymonoline.com*)

It is telling that our present-day usage of the word did not begin until the Industrial Revolution was well on its way to terra-forming our planet and all its inhabitants. But make no mistake: we are absolutely fascinated by the word 'apocalypse' but more to the point we are fascinated with our species' own death throes and ultimate demise. Look no further than the social silo of modern pop culture. The birth of our modern fascination begins here in pop culture and if there is a beginning of our culture's public conversation about the apocalypse you could argue that it began in 1916 with a Danish film entitled *The End of the World (Verdens Undergang)* with its planet-wide disasters and social upheaval being triggered by a near-miss from a passing comet. But in my eyes the actual beginning, the monumental event in the pop-culture fascination with the Apocalypse was the Halloween radio broadcast 8 pm Eastern time on October 30, 1938, narrated and directed by Orson Wells. Many listeners mistook this radio show as an actual, factual live report of such an invasion. This was revealing to our enemies how gullible and naïve the American public was but also opened the floodgate to conspiracy theories about aliens and a sinister government cover-up. It also showed the growing entertainment industry in Hollywood that there was money to be made to depict the terror and the violence that lurks in the collective consciousness of our young species.

From there you have an endless (and I mean endless) supply of cinema and TV movies depicting nuclear holocaust, over-population, and environmental collapse to zombie apocalypse. Let's just look at cinema for a moment starting with *When Worlds Collide (1951), On the Beach (1959), Dr. Strangelove (1964), Night of the Living Dead (1968), Planet of the Apes (1968), Omega Man (1971), Silent Running (1972), Soylent Green (1973), A Boy and His Dog (1975), Dawn of the Dead (1978), Apocalypse Now (1979), The Road Warrior (1981), The Day After (1983), The Terminator (1984), Nausicaa of the Valley of the Wind (1984), The Quiet Earth (1985), When the Wind Blows (1986), Aliens (1986), They Live (1988), Delicatessen (1991), Waterworld (1995), Independence Day (1996), Armageddon (1998), Deep Impact (1998), The Matrix (1999), 28 Days Later (2002), The Day After Tomorrow (2004), Shaun of the Dead (2004), War of the Worlds (2005), Children of Men (2006), I Am Legend (2007), Pontypool (2008), Cloverfield (2008), Wall-E (2008), Pandorum (2009), Zombieland (2009), The Road (2009), 9 (2009), The Book of Eli (2010), The Crazies (2010), Legion (2010), Zombie Apocalypse (2011), Take Shelter (2011), Contagion (2011), Prometheus (2012), Snowpiercer (2013), World War Z (2013), The World's End (2013), Mad Max: Fury Road (2015), Z for Zachariah (2015), Train to Busan (2016), It Comes At Night (2017), War for the Planet of the Apes (2017), The Quiet Place (2018), Knock At the Cabin (2023), Leave the World Behind (2023),* …this list goes on and on.

Our fascination with our species' own demise is endless. Why? Can it be that as a species, collectively we see it coming? As if 65 million years ago, the dinosaurs collectively sensed the hurtling of the asteroid toward their lush and vibrant home in the Yucatan with a mere 11 minutes for them to say, 'I told you so.' Can it be that a new age is truly dawning and all our fascination with alien abductions and visitations are really a projection of this imminent, spiritual event upon the collective heart of humanity? Can it be that collectively we are sensing a cataclysmic plague about to infect humanity, causing all but a few chosen survivors to be doomed to wander about the land as feral animals returning to a previous lower state of existence? Why this fascination with the end? Is the grand experiment over? Can it really be that our sleepy, violent species intuitively knows the end is near and our movie writers and directors are the neo-Jeremiah's and Issaiah's? Do those who command the visual arts with movies, videos, and social media command the collective spirit of our species? Has our technology created an artificial, planetary nous (what Teilard de Chardin nailed when he called it the 'Noosphere') tightly wrapping us in its staticky embrace? Have we found a way to replicate the spiritual with our technology? Have we done it?

One of the primary messages of the 4th Way movement and the teachings of G.I. Gurdjieff and P.D. Ouspensky and Boris Mouravieff is that without great effort, humanity is a species asleep. We *Homo Sapiens* are somnambulists walking through our existence at the mercy of cosmic forces designed to keep us asleep. Very, very few of us truly wake up to the reality of God incarnate within our psyche. And we get to the end of our days, and we realize we've just been watching a movie of our life, not really participating in any of it. We've just gone about our time here, wasting it on silly and useless daydreaming in pursuit of petty desires and needs which only feed into our ultimate return to this planet or some other 'place' to go through this life again and again.

Unless we apply mighty energy and mighty efforts toward awakening while we are here on this planet then we are doomed to loop back around and have another go at it. Without these enormous efforts while we are here in this secret school then we just let others dream for us, placing our confused and chaotic whimpering about the apocalypse onto the silver screen for us. We pathetically sigh 'yes' as we fumble for the keys on the way to the car in the cinema parking lot. We go home, fall asleep and dream of being enrolled into a secret school yet when the morning comes that dream fades like a light fog and we forget who we are: Children of Light. We forget our birthright and are expelled from the Garden of Eden. Our existence is reduced to a struggle to regain this access to the 'Garden.' We spend our time here trying to remember our cosmic origin. It is our cosmic job to reclaim our birthright. It is your cosmic job to reclaim your birthright. You are a child of light.

Without great efforts we are wasting our education in this secret school. We must work diligently at remembering our birthright. Firstly, a command post must be created within our psyche. The elders of this Secret School call this a 'magnetic center.' It is a 'fort' if you will, (roughly located (if you must have a physical location) in and around the Pineal Gland buried deep inside the human brain. This fort was established to learn how to observe and defend against what are called 'A' influences. These influences are the source of all which plague us, and by 'all', I mean 'ALL.' You must learn how to overcome them by discerning them from other influences. These other influences are called B, C, D and E influences. They are the source of your evolution, the source of your salvation and life-giving energy. You must learn how to separate these from the A influences. This learning how to separate these influences is where the difficulty lies. It takes years of work on oneself, beginning to know and understand this process of spiritual evolution is based on 'grace.' You cannot manipulate this esoteric evolution with cheap methods found on a YouTube Short or manipulative techniques based in desires of the changing masks you constantly wear. This path that we speak of here is based on patience and endurance and courage all fueled by gratitude and acceptance and joy.

You must learn how to discern…discern what is you and what isn't you.

This psychological fort or command post is neither started by you nor can you build it. As Brian McQueen says, you must get "baptized and begin the work commonly known as the struggle against sin. The sin/confession/repentance process is the machinery to gain the grace to build and strengthen the magnetic center." The Esoteric Circle or our secret school was established to educate those 'who have ears to hear.' Intense psychological work must be done while 'there is daylight' to pass the tests of this school we call 'life on Earth.' Intense work must be completed to gain the privilege of not returning the Earth.

The irony is (unless you are among the 'just' who are born of a 'virgin') it takes an extensive period of purification to arrive at a place of awakening (many times returning to Earth for another go at being released from your Karmic Burden). Those who are initiated into this secret school (from other dimensions teeming with life) here on Earth go through a lifetime of remembering and detoxing from our past, karmic build-up. Some of us graduate from this secret school, yet never realize this until our physical body releases itself to the laws governed by this world. All the while we are guided by the unseen spirit worlds teeming with life un-ending. This unseen, spiritual world is everlasting and eternal, permanent, and pre-existent. But to the ordinary, unchanged, common world, this reality is invisible and mysterious. Cinema and film again do the spiritual exploration for us for us depicting this unseen world as demons penetrating this world, lurking in the shadows of our Stephen King dreamscape. This secret school teaches us how to evolve out of our feral, animalistic existence. It teaches us how to evolve into the divine beings we are designed to be, utilizing this secret school as a purification station shedding our divine spark of its personal and collective karmic burden. This reality calls to us, all of us. Very few answered this call.

This is the call which you have been hearing all your born days…the call of the secret school, the Esoteric Circle. Will you answer it?

# Chapter One:
# What is the Esoteric Circle?

## YouTube and the Pandemic

Welcome to the Esoteric Circle. My name is Pete Haskins. Wherever you are on your spiritual journey, blessings to you. You are welcome here. This is a safe space to talk about your spiritual journey.

What an epic time to be alive, huh?! What a time indeed...the time of planetary transition, which means every living thing on our planet will be answering the same questions: who am I? Why am I here? How do I survive this transition? How do I evolve?

If you're reading this, you're probably preparing to have or are having your spiritual awakening. I want to welcome you here. On the surface this book is a companion piece to my Esoteric Circle Youtube channel (@esotericcircle4364) which I began on April 7, 2020, during the Covid-19 lockdown. However, this book is primarily a celebration of *your* own spiritual journey during one of the most horrifying and spectacularly exciting times in the history of our wayward and young species.

This book will hopefully be a companion to you on

your journey as we both share with one another the insights we have gathered on this monumental investigation we call an 'Esoteric Journey.' It is by no means a complete guide to your spiritual awakening. There has never been a book ever written that is a complete guide to anyone's spiritual awakening. Even the Judeo-Christian Bible leaves out the 'how?" There are books that come close though, but nothing can relate completely to you and your own Karmic history to feed you on every psychic level. Books are just signposts giving out general directions and distances, hints and suggestions supplying us all with needed checklists for the journey ahead. When it comes right down to it, this journey must mimic our journey into death where we are to answer for our own time on this planet. This is an individual journey toward the afterlife.

This book is designed and written to be a companion for you, without being immersed in doctrine and dogma. This book will discuss old ideas and concepts and authors as well as possibly introducing you to new ideas and authors along the way. In other words, this book is an exploration...an investigation into our collective past. This book is also an invitation to you to begin or to continue your own exploration and investigation into *your* own past, your own present and your own future.

Each one of us is a unique creature gifted with hidden talents, but for us to realize our purpose in life and eventually fulfill our cosmic destiny and move past this Earthly prison we must 'unpack' our physiological and spiritual Karmic burden. This takes time, valuable time to unpack your inherited and personal burden. Your spiritual evolution isn't obtained, purchased, or captured. It is accepted, as the Earth accepts the life-giving rains and the cleansing fires both with the same Spirit of gratitude and grace.

**Attention is the golden gift**

Your attention is your only tool on this inward journey. It's not a weapon to storm the 'gates of heaven.' Attention is the golden gift. You must learn how to utilize it, allowing it to open the gate of awareness within you so that the grace of God can flow through you. The embryonic Logos within your sleepy soul won't be pursued like just another weight loss program, or a rush of dopamine or melatonin shot or a DMT hit. This is not a trivial 'New Age' gimmick inspired by a sick society which can be downloaded like some free app on your iPhone. Using modern technology has the potential to be a blessing or a curse. If not used carefully it can steal the spiritual content of the message as technology is primarily designed to quicken and streamline any activity you aim it at, like a weapon. The Spiritual Journey is no different. One must be very careful not to fall into the trap that this ancient, Esoteric path should be modernized via social media and Artificial Intelligence and modern technology just for the sake of being more spiritually efficient. Our age is burdened by arrogance in our technological marvels. We use algorithms as our handmade brick and sludge as we build our own version of the Tower of Babel.

This book is about the 'old school' style of the spiritual journey. It is the Hero's Journey and the mythology which surrounds it, sustains it, and enlivens it. It is not a book for the 'porch' Christians, you know, those people who just want the outward appearance of religion. It is not a book for those who want a quick fixed approach to their spiritual development. This book is for those who are interested in the hero's journey, the journey which leads toward a state of permanent grace…a journey which leads toward salvation. The journey toward reclaiming your birthright as a child of light.

Yet this book also seeks to translate those old themes and teachings into the modern language, making the old relevant to this brave new world we inhabit. This book isn't about 'throwing the baby out with the bathwater,' as the old saying goes. Many folks who are interested in a post-Christian spiritual journey are ready to start from 'scratch.' I think that is a mistake. If we are to have a successful journey and reach 'Theosis' or 'Divinization,' then we need to re-establish our link with our collective wisdom yet dive deeply into our own individual psyche and discover the new 'balm' or remedy to balance our unstable society. The key to a spiritual awakening which leads to permanence is realizing that you should remain linked to the Esoteric Circle, that ancient, perfect circle of spiritual wisdom which has been passed down through the ages to us, is still accessible. But only through our individual, purely human psyche. Our collective spiritual evolution will only be valid if it is a pure link to this perfect, Esoteric Circle. The way we re-connect with this Esoteric Circle is to dive deeply into our own individual lives, unpacking and clearing away the psychic debris of the past and wait to be filled with the 'new wine.'

This spiritual journey you are on is all about you diving deeply into your own psyche away from all the 'A' Influences which this Oubliette of a planet produces like toxic gas from a coal-fired power plant. You are on a hero's journey. You. This is all about you. We must be 'born again' as Christ says. This being *born again* **is** the Hero's Journey. It is Esoteric Science grounded in thousands and thousands of years of psychological teachings handed down through generations of monks and shamans and priests of countless orders and sects and secret societies and Mystery Schools. It is not accessible simply through a YouTube subscription, a book purchase, an ice bath, a new crystal, or a new breathing technique. There is a price, a psychological price, far beyond what most people are willing to pay. There is your own personal cross to bear, to ascend upon and die to your old, Karmic selves. You must have your own Golgotha. If you are not willing to face this test, then your spiritual journey should be called something else.

To inherit your spiritual destiny and be children of Light you must remove the past psychic trauma and experiences and influences which are holding you back on your evolutionary path. As the French Jesuit Pierre Teilhard de Chardin prophesied, the next evolutionary step for humanity is psychic in nature, not physiological. We must be born again as Christ tells Nicodemus in John 3, "So don't be surprised when I tell you that you must be 'born from above'- out of this world, so to speak. You know well enough how the wind blows this way and that. You hear it rustling through the trees, but you have no idea where it comes from or where it's headed next. That's the way it is with everyone 'born from above' by the wind of God, the Spirit of God."

Christ has been my guide, but I must move my own spiritual 'feet' and work while it is daylight at my own spiritual/psychic evolution. No one (not even Christ) can walk for me. Same goes for you. You have an inherited and personal Karmic burden which must be unpacked and discarded. Obstacles must be removed, overcome, ignored, fought, and destroyed for you to successfully reach 'Theosis.' It is this hero's journey which we must all take if we are serious about serving God and serving the Cosmos as an open and loving Child of Light. You are on a hero's journey. You and no one else. This is all about you and your birthright.

### Charles Ashanin, Robin Amis and das Schloss

Regarding the Youtube channel, my sole purpose in producing these little videos was to share what had been shared with me about Esoteric Christianity from two Holy men I had met on my journey; the first man was a Montenegran mystic named Charles Bozidar Ashanin (aka Bozidar Asanin) and the second an English Nobleman named Robin Amis. Together they introduced me to the hidden, inner truth about Christianity, namely that there was indeed a lost Christianity (as Jacob Needleman called it) which mirrored Raja Yoga and Zen Buddhism and the Sufis of Islam. Through the twists and turns of a thousand years of history since the Great Schism of 1054 CE when the Church of Rome decided to divorce itself from the original teachings contained within the heart of Christianity seated in the East, in Constantinople (modern day Istanbul, Turkey), this teaching

21

had been lost (or at least muted to the point of a faint whisper) to the West.

To make matters worse, when the Protestant Church broke off from the Catholic Church in the 16th Century (all in the ironic reason of a deeper access to God via Holy Scripture) then truly the traces of this inner tradition were reduced to a near dead-silence as any vibrations of sound of this inner tradition were isolated to one geographic spot on this oubliette, we call home: Mount Athos in Greece. Consequently, those of us in the West were cut off from our Spiritual inheritance of this inner tradition and all that was left was a two-dimensional religion completely immersed in the ethically based, shallow, outward imitation of right moral behavior. Our religion (the etymology of the word 'religion' means literally to "re-link with God") was horribly distorted and contaminated and left to slowly decay as its power to function as an authentic world religion was essentially removed, leaving it unable to do what a true religion does: prepare the soul to pass-over to the afterlife. This preparation comes with a cost, a sacrifice, a personal cross to bear yet we in the Protestant and Catholic tradition have been fooled into thinking that this long-awaited salvation which we seek is 'universal' and takes no more sacrifice on our part other than blind obedience to a Pope or a club membership in the right church drenched in the right politics and doctrine with the only sacrifice being two-fold: firstly, the outward imitation of certain moral behavior and secondly, the suspension of any personal pursuit of one's own bliss.

Essentially, to be a modern Christian in the West in the early 21st Century requires no thinking at all…it's all a game of imitation…no training, no preparation, no suffering, no repentance, no passion, no compassion, no wonderment, no knowledge, no understanding…no hero's journey…just do what everyone else is doing and you'll be fine. It's all a joke, like Kafka's unfinished and last novel 'The Castle' ('Das Schloss') where our hero named simply 'K.' tries and tries to obtain entry into the Castle and speak to those in charge but he cannot gain access. This is a perfect example of Christianity today where we have the goal but no way to obtain it.

There's no other choice really…no one within the ranks of the Protestant and Catholic as well as the rank and file of the typical Orthodox tradition knows any different. The core of this inner teaching of Christianity has been lost to human history…or has it?

Then what hope does one have outside of the boundaries of accepted Christian dogma and doctrine? We are feverishly searching for answers which don't require much inward motion and work. We look to Terrence McKenna as a modern bearded prophet with amazingly articulate and inspiring talks on YouTube about the Stoned Ape, micro-dosing Psilocybin mushrooms and the next step in the evolutionary journey of the species known as *homo sapiens.* YouTube is littered with answer after answer by people all telling us that God is a frequency or an Alien reptile or an Anunnaki who can be accessed simply by decalcifying the Pineal Gland or habitually dying and being reborn in ice bath after ice bath or meditating with a certain tone (420 hz?) flowing through your salvific ipods which automatically propel you onto the next stage of your spiritual journey or whatever the method may be which has been fed to you by the YT or TikTok algorithm. On and on these hacks and shortcuts are merchandized on YouTube, which has become a virtual street corner where success is determined by views and monetization. Social media has made spiritual development into a cheap game played by Capitalists masquerading as spiritual gurus. It's all a joke, just as Jesus found the Temple before he cleared it of money changers and charlatans.

Where do we find the way into 'das Schloss'?

For Christianity (of any flavor) there's only one geographic place where this inner tradition remains: Mount Athos peninsula in Greece. Yet there is more hope…this tradition remains alive not just in the 20+ monasteries on the rocky coast of Greece but more importantly in the few people left on this Earth who carry this tradition, this inner tradition of Early Christianity within the 'womb of their nous.' These are modern-day Apostles who have used their earthly existence to carry this message of the inner tradition to the Western Church. This book is inspired by the message of two Apostles who carried this message to searchers like our selves: Charles Ashanin and Robin Amis. These men were two such saints who spent their lives sharing this message of the inner church to anyone who had ears to listen.

### Listen, but not too hard

I listened too hard and now there is no going back for me. I must share this message with you. I have no choice but to share it with you and I want to thank you for listening this far. Be careful not to listen too hard my friend. There is no going back after these secrets are whispered into the inner chamber of your psyche, the vibrations unlocking the seat of your soul and you are finally awakened to the life you were meant to live…a life unencumbered by the restraints of a dying civilization quickly succumbing to the violence and decadence it has encouraged for far too long now. For now it is too late to turn back as our civilization is descending into the abyss of chaos and anarchy where the pearls of our wisdom are spilled out into the pig's trough and mixed in with the slop…the bottom-feeders gulping it up and reducing it to common waste, into the nothingness of a culture which has forgotten its roots and heritage, consuming its garbage and lapping up its own vomit.

This book you're reading right now has one purpose: to gather up those of us who have ears to hear. A call for the circle to form again, as if for battle. A call for the formation of this ancient of circles as the storm is already upon us.

As Jesus Christ warned, this esoteric teaching contained within the Gospels is not for everyone. It is for those of us who have ears to hear. This form of spiritual hearing is a developed skill. To develop this spiritual hearing, it must be passed on by a member of this Esoteric Circle. Charles Ashanin and Robin Amis were two such members. I am now passing their influence onto you and inviting you to be a part of this Esoteric Circle. I am inviting you to remember.

This book and my YT channel will share key influences (called C and D influences by the Esoteric Brotherhood) from certain members of our society who have quietly shared this knowledge with the world. Now as we move into a new age (the Age of the Holy Spirit, the age of Aquarius or whatever you would like to call it) all the previous held rules of sharing this Esoteric knowledge are thrown out the proverbial window as the worldly A influences are spilling out into the nooks and crannies of the spirit world and we who do have ears to hear have nowhere to hide.  We have no Athos monastery to run to, no Annie Dillard-mountain creek to trek to and hunker down into some cabin.  Even the rain that falls from heaven contains micro-bits of plastic as a sinister sign of how far-reaching our sick society has reached in its violence and decay.  The world is quite literally burning and drowning and we're still arguing whether Climate Change is real or not…amazing.  There are no more horizons, literally.  8.8 billion of us looking for a spiritual 'hand' but the Gandalfs and Obi-Wans and Neos are all gone, and we are left to crawl out of the Oubliette on our own…

…or are we on our own?  No, not quite…. there is help in finding your way out of this darkness…let's talk for a bit…

### What is the Esoteric Circle?

Caveat Emptor: this shaded pathway into the depth of God, the deep dark woods mark time beside the rotten signposts which stands before you, inviting you, beckoning you and anyone like you to take the next monumental step. Yet suddenly you realize there are no destinations on the post, bits of white paint flick off with the wind into the timeless way.  No direction saves your instinct now…what'll it be? Which way to go?

This dark and lonely pathway is open to anyone, of course...offered to anyone...yet the bitter truth remains it is meant for a few and that is what excites you and frightens you. You want to be special, unique...an undiscovered gem on the creek bed ready to be discovered...but once the steps have been taken and you are lost for the first time...and it is night fall and you have no idea where you are (and all the trees look the same in this twilight) and there is no one to guide...then you want the comfort of two-dimensional, vanilla life of an hourly worker waiting for the next commercial and then: bedtime...and tomorrow the same and the same and the same until your body dies and the Universe performs (what Boris Mouravieff calls) an astral abortion and you fade into nothing. (so, it was true this talk of simulation)

Jesus warned you, didn't he? He warned us all and we all know this...but I thought he was speaking in metaphor...well, not all the time apparently...Jesus remarks that the gate is narrow, and few are those who make it through (Mt 7: 13-14, John 10: 1-3,7, 9). This Esoteric Circle is a small circle, created to be the core of our civilized world containing the teaching which is preserved to remind and rekindle the inner divinity which makes us who we are, something higher than an insect or an animal...we are divine...yet we forget and need to remember.

P.D. Ouspensky writes in his essay 'Esotericism and Modern Thought,' that *"the esoteric circle is, as it were, humanity, within humanity, and is the brain, or rather the immortal soul, of humanity, where all the attainments, all the results, all the achievements, of all cultures and all civilizations are preserved."*

I will define the Esoteric Circle as this*: the Esoteric Circle is a protective, singularly focused clan of homo sapiens whose cosmic job is to assist in the preservation of the psychological teachings of true humanity. These teachings are designed to delicately lead individual humans out of their feral condition, teaching each of them the art of releasing personal and inherited karma and being twice born into its permanent, deified state of salvation.* [This will be the working definition of 'Esoteric Circle' for the remainder of this book]

## Stranger in a Strange Land

It is a lonely path that will keep you on the outside of acceptable civilization. You will be a stranger to the world, living outside the comfortable confines of acceptable civilization which is today riddled with so much barbarism that it's hardly distinguishable from a brutal pack of wild, feral humans living from day to day huddled around a pitiful flame is some dank stinky cave. You'll no longer be ok with just fitting in with the usual goals of education, partying, making a living, raising a family, saving for retirement and being excited about lowering your cholesterol or making it through your first colonoscopy or finally paying off your Honda Odyssey. You'll realize that you've never fit it into your social setting, into your family, into your community, into your society, into your civilization. You'll have odd traits and characteristics which are antiquated or just plain odd which set you out from your peers in school or work or family. You'll realize this and eventually be led into the realization that you are not 'from' here.

Your pre-existent self is a stranger in a strange land. It is a blessed day indeed when you realize this during your lifetime. If you do realize this, it is time to move on from your inherited past and begin to live in true freedom. In **Genesis 23: 3-4,** Moses writes, 'Then Abraham rose from before his dead, and spoke to the sons of Heth, saying, "I am a stranger and a sojourner among you; give me a burial site among you that I may bury my dead out of sight."' We are strangers here in this place. We need to remember this, bury our past lives while we are awake in this body. Then and only then are we allowed to move on, never to return to this present form.

Some of us will have the skies opened for us and the generative principle will be slowly revealed. But this is dangerous territory. We need to have help from those who are working on our behalf from the other side. There is always corresponding activity occurring in a mirrored world.

We call these beings 'angels,' for lack of a better word. Each one of us assigned to a 'guardian angel.' Most of us are connected to our guardian angel through a blood line, i.e. grandfather or aunt or great grandmother. This common blood acts as a conduit or receiver for spiritual energy, allowing for communication beyond comprehension. This blood literally connects us with the 'other' side if we only have ears to hear. This connection is established by 'august beings that rise to higher planes of existence by sacrificing their own substances,' as Rudolph Steiner says in *The Gospel of St. John and its Relation to the other Gospels*. This life is a reconnection with these higher sources. Our job here on this planet is to learn how to listen.

# Chapter Two:
## You are on the hero's journey

### Spiritual Homeland

The call of the journey waits for no one. You either go or you don't. You pay the price either way. But a warning to the wise: You won't feel like you're home until you are truly, truly on your own Odyssey and you are your own Ulysses trying to make it home again…home again in that spiritual sense of the word where you are united with your Maker and you take a look around you and say yes…this is what I've been dreaming of all along…was my life on Earth just a dream that I was slowly climbing out of, lifetime after lifetime ascending to the place that I was before and struggling to make it past that marker and into the open space free from my old Karma weighing me down and preventing me from finding true freedom?

You (if you are a true member of the Esoteric Circle) have always been on a mission to return to your place of cosmic origin. If you are a member of this ancient circle, then you are not and have never really been comfortable with this life. You've never really 'fit in' have you…although you've tried…you've tried desperately to fit in to society, but you've always felt like you're a stranger in a strange landscape, as if you were alone on a strange planet dwelling amongst a strange people. You've never fit in. And this brings us together here, speaking together through the pages of this book...

This book will be a guide for you, a substitute until you meet a master of the Circle who can truly lead you deeper into this journey. If you've picked up this book and read this far, that's a good sign you're remembering something familiar. This book will introduce or better still, re-introduce you to old ideas which you somehow find familiar, their energy resonating through your inner sanctuary like choral voices ringing through the stalls of Chartres...this book will feed you with the hope that you aren't alone, that you are indeed on a path of awakening to your true purpose on this planet. This book can be a source of fine energies for you, pointing you in the direction of other books, other authors, other ideas so that you can advance on...on toward your next stage. And if you haven't already, this book will help guide you toward a group as well as a master teacher. You cannot progress on this Esoteric path without a group and without a master teacher.

If this sounds familiar to you...if you remember this in some strange way...then welcome...welcome to the pathway that you have been on for a long, long time already. On this path, as you take a step forward remember this: each step forward is an enormous victory. Each step. With each step forward you will be met with help from the other side, beckoning you to take another and then another. This is the law of synergia which states that as God has taken the initial step through the life and sacrifice of Jesus Christ, you are constantly invited to take the next step. When you do, God automatically takes another step toward you…then you are invited to take another, and God reacts and so on and so on…this is the build-up of what Pierre Teilhard de Chardin termed 'radial' energy as opposed to 'tangential' energy. Radial energy moves toward the center, building up and sustaining itself, whereas tangential energy moves from the center to the outside, losing its energy through entropy, like the burning of a log on a fire, never able to retrieve that energy once it has been burned. This cosmic, spiritual energy is not like that…it gains energy with its movement toward evolution of the being, carrying its energy toward the spiritual propagation of this cosmic species.

As you gain the necessary energy needed to see through the haze of your karmic burden you will realize something. Your homeland is spiritual and not geographic. Time after time human beings get this wrong and countless wars upon wars have been fought over just this very issue: mistaking the spiritual homeland with the geographic location here on this terrestrial planet. Human beings equate their true spiritual origin with the place of their birth, the place where their 'race' fought battle after battle, war after war to secure as if it were a physical portal to their true homeland.

Your true spiritual homeland is not some place here on Earth. It is within you, there to be re-discovered during this lifetime that you have been given. You must work diligently to re-discover how to re-open this cosmic portal that is within you so you can return to your true origin. Charles Ashanin said this to me before his earthly death: "Those people who think that this world is all there is so wrong. There are other worlds out there teeming with life."

## The Cosmic Value of Friendship

My connection to the Inner Church was through a mystic named Bozidar Asanin, or Charles Ashanin as his Western friends knew him. He and Robin Amis are the only reason we are speaking right now, the only reason. They intervened in my life and said: there is more to life than daydreaming!

Charles in particular, whose home I visited at 5329 Boulevard Place in Indianapolis, Indiana every Wednesday at 4 pm for 5 years as I began my arduous journey. We would have English tea (with a little bit of sugar) and I would sit and listen to his stories about his home of Montenegro (which he had been exiled from since he was 24 years old, and he escaped Tito's Communist thugs and made it to Italy in 1944...then England...then Scotland...then Ghana and then finally America). He taught me much but nothing more valuable than the importance of cosmic friendship.

In a taped interview he did with a Buddhist friend of his named Bob Colson on Dec 10, 1999 (just before Charles's Earthly death on March 1, 2000) in which he spoke of the equality of friendship on this esoteric level. Essentially the Christ in me greets the Christ in you, reuniting to cells of the cosmic body of Christ at that point in time. This friendship is based not only on the mutual attraction of the two personalities (this term 'personality' is used here loosely and regards the general term for everyone and not the 'Personality' often used within the language of Esotericism) who meet as two equals in every way (socio-economic, etc.) but also on a deeper, inner (esoteric) level. Spirit meets Spirit. Deep meets deep. Love meets love...and the two reunited cells re-emerge as one. This act is as Teilhard de Chardin pointed out radial in nature instead of tangential.  In other words, the energy created between two truly equal friends creates an energy which draws the energy of the two personalities inward (radial) creating a build-up of that energy, creating more of it…and still more of it as the love for one another builds and builds, multiplying the strength of both.  This inward motion draws in energy, sending out a beacon into the darkness of the freezing cosmos that two long-lost cells have reunited, calling on the attention of this quietly active, 'heavenly' realm to give them attention and send them even more energy.  This reunification attracts this heavenly energy, adding to it an unearthly quality, which no human can destroy, no bond to be broken, no conflict too great to tear their friendship apart because the connection between the two is more, much more than just getting along with one another and enjoying the same hobby or watching sports together or fishing or yoga or knitting or pickle ball or cooking or whatever it may be.  This attraction between you and your friend goes deep, cosmically deep.

Be not mistaken by this: friendships on this level are rare, rare indeed.  If you experience one during your time on this planet, then you are blessed.  These rare relationships are meant to be treated with great care, making sure the relationship continues multiple levels as it continues to be a conduit, an avenue, a thoroughfare for the unearthly energies which began this motion in the first place. True friendships are an unearthly treasure for you. It is a reunification of nothing more than the cosmic body of Christ experienced in this life between two *homo sapiens*. We are the species designed to carry this spark of the Eternal within the tiny chamber in the center of our grey matter, centered in the third eye (the tiny, hollowed area between the Pituitary and Pineal Gland). This is the seat of God, the sanctuary of the soul, the chamber of the Highest, the gate to awareness of the Holy, if you must know a location, which we in the West seem to be obsessed with...one of these rare friendships can spark this awakening of the third eye. It is what Mouravieff refers to as the kindred spirit of the polar beings in his *Gnosis Trilogy*.

There is nothing that can pull this relationship of love apart, except the pettiness of negative emotions from the lower, uncouth emotional center which lay at the surface of every Westerner: jealousies and fear and anger...when they get all tangled up in blue (as Bob Dylan says). Indeed, these types of friendships are not 'set in stone.' But all emotions are merely distortions of the one and only true emotion: love, right? They must be tended, protected, and kept pure as if your life depended on it, utilizing the sense of loyalty as your lighthouse during the storms which occur as this friendship is attacked by negative emotions which naturally occur in this fallen world of ours. But a true cosmic friendship is not of this world. Mark this as true. When you discover this fact, you will know what I mean as this friendship will become a guiding light for you in the darkest of times. Know this: the darkness will come and you will need a friend, on this side as well as on the other side to help guide you through the maze of your karma, this burden which we all carry (with the exception of the pure in heart, those 'once' born into this world with no karmic burden like Jesus Christ and Siddhartha and Mary Magdalene…true Christian friendship is to be treasured above all relationships that you will ever have upon this Earth.

Our 'post-modern' era of friendship can be quite dysfunctional…especially throughout social media. More specifically relationships and friendships on YouTube and Instagram and Facebook can be terribly transactional in nature. That is, they can be based on an investment by someone with attention through time and likes and comments and subscriptions, etc. but only based on an expectation of a return on that investment. This is where our capitalistic mentality pervades our spiritual thought process, creating a toxic foundational layer of thought at the basis of our online activities.

In an Esoteric Friendship (we'll capitalize it here even though it is not a formal name of any one friendship) you give that person attention (through the psychic nature of your love/energy) without any expectation of any return on your 'investment.' Make no mistake, friendships are an investment but not in any transactional sense. These Esoteric Friendships are organic in nature, their composition being made of the stuff of the stars just as much as any other creation. This composition contains the deep, dark secrets of the far-off places which can only be envisioned within the eye of the soul, being activated like a beacon sending out signals of rare alchemical particles of rare form of love and grace and mercy and hope. You are receiving (as in a gift) something quite remarkable in this Esoteric Friendship: you are receiving (as it were) a message from another world that there is help on its way to assist you on your journey. You are receiving a boost of fine energies which originate from 'on high' which assist you on your journey out of this Oubliette. You are receiving a new source of rare and alchemical energy (what we can only call 'love') which you breathe in and pull up into the area around your Pineal Gland so that it mixes and merges with the already present energy that you are born with. This commixture of love is what happens during a holy communion experience when that wine is indeed changed into the 'blood' of Christ so that essentially an Esoteric Friendship is another 'room' that is attached to the sacrifice of Christ, giving us access to the additional energy we need to continue our journey on this planet, in this atmosphere.

Otherwise, this atmosphere that we are born into is really an atmosphere of terror where negative emotions of all shapes and sizes rule us as slaves. We do indeed need another ally with us to help inject into our physical nature a new alchemical reaction which will enhance and guide us in this vast darkness that is this existence. I mean no wonder we have had such a hard time in this existence! There are so many opportunities to 'fall off' as it were…to get lost on this trail because the nature of this strange land that we are born into is full of darkness which is not just the absence of light, but more importantly it is a new substance, an actual physical element which the physicists cannot describe, namely 'dark matter' which in some estimates composes the vast majority of all the matter within the 'known' Universe.

### How????

At the beginning of my spiritual awakening my question was/is this: the Bible only tells us what this transformation *looks like* but does not tell us *how* to get to this spiritual condition. Where is the HOW? This 'how' is the subject of this book. One of the most significant drawbacks or negative aspects to modern Christianity in the 21st Century is the lack of a scientific method which can be applied to the inner life. I'm not speaking of 'scientific' in the modern medicine sort of way. I'm talking about something completely different. I'm talking about a replicable method for the inner life so that permanence can be developed. This is the missing piece of the puzzle! Why can't the stuff in the Gospels be replicated?! Where is it and how can I have access to it? In other words: HOW?

There *is* a 'how,' but this knowledge is both lost and hidden at the same time. Who would think to look for the Christ in a damp and stinky cave in backwater Bethlehem, right? But who would think to look for the spark of God within an animal, just learning to walk upright?

You must work for this knowledge and earn your understanding and develop savoir faire (the ability to 'do' and be purposeful and functional). You don't just wake up one morning and say, 'I'd like to be a member of the Esoteric Circle,' like you've found a new app you heard about. This is amazingly serious business here with a cosmic element underlying everything that is being spoken of…the frequency of the very thought of this within your mind has to be familiar and haunting…the very thought of this 'esoteric circle' or this inner life or meditation…when you think of this subject there must be a frequency to the thought which reverberates into your mind so deeply, with such familiarity that you pause, a strange heatless heat rises in your solar plexus and begins to move toward the crown of your head and you have communication without comprehension about the whispering of angels which you are hearing, the silent muttering of the angel into your inner heart, telling you yes…yes this is the way…this is the way…this is the hero's journey.

This is where Joseph Campbell and his teaching on the Hero Journey comes into play. You are essentially on a hero's journey, that epic journey which is reserved for the gods and the heroes of myth and legend. You are meant to be the new Ulysses, Prometheus, Odin and the Obi-Wan Kenobi…you are meant to be the Gandalf and Neo, the Mary Magdalene and the Jesus Christ of your own soul who confronts the thousand faces of your own reflection in the ancient pool you find in the middle earth of your psyche where your grandest enemy is you. The wildest beast that threatens to burn your crops and kill your family and horde your gold is you…you must face that enemy of the self and allow the death of that old self to occur within the coldness of your darkest night and you…you must await your own resurrection…the resurrection of the ancients where time has no pull nor place…you must become the god you search for by refusing to become the God you search for…that is the twist…the becoming only happens when the crown is refused and death is chosen, sacrifice and bliss, terror and ecstasy…love and horror…passion and rage all inhabit the same home, living in a harmony which rises above the dangers and destruction of language and definition and time.

Duality falls away like the dead skin of the snake that sheds its skin at the right time, only at the right time. You are neither darkness nor light…you are both, hung, blending, and mixing in the air above the pool that floats above the doorway to reunion with the source of it all…the source of our life, our strength, our love. This hero's journey is the journey of our Fathers and Mothers…all of those ancestors who we never knew yet have always heard, whispering to us in our half-waking dreams curled under a blanket, thinking nothing of it…it was just a dream, just a dream…it was nothing you tell yourself, now go back to sleep…you have many promises to keep and miles to go…your entire life has been lived on the edge of knowing, the edge of knowing what your purpose really was but you were always so busy and so worried and so focused on what you couldn't reach, what you couldn't understand, what you didn't have…but now time grows short and the nights are long and you still have these lingering thoughts: there is more…there is more that beckons me…what is it? What is it that beckons me? Could it be that I am the hero that I have long been searching for? Could it be that the authors and the musicians and movie stars are the very reflections of myself all along? All along have I contained the elements of my own salvation within these dreams that I have convinced myself are nothing and add up to nothing? Are my own desires and dreams really letters from the Almighty telling me to push further into the dark woods?  Push further…leave your home and follow the pathless path where monsters and demons lurk behind the mercury smooth Beech trees standing as silent witnesses of so many strange sights.

Could it be that you are literally…*literally* a vital portal to another Universe, another reality which leads our species to the next step on its journey through the darkest night of our existence?  Could it be that you are a doorway and all your life you've been waiting for this moment to be opened like an ancient gate to a vault inscribed with fantastic scenes of strange creatures and messages of instruction and warning and hope?  Could it be that you contain within you the key pathway back to the place of your origin?  All this while thinking that God was in a book or in a church or in a song when all the while he was in your mind, and you just needed to figure out how to find God?  Yes.  It is all here, and you are on this journey of a lifetime, a lifetime of lifetimes back to the place of your origin. This is the journey you are on.  This is the fantastic journey which you must take alone and in the shelter of your own soul…indeed your soul serving as the ancient doorway to the inner world you have been seeking all along…that journey which leads us out of the darkness of our soul's winter solstice and into the light of your true spiritual homeland.

## Finding the Right Frequency in the absurdity of time

It's really all about finding the right frequency in your spiritual life. (Is it as simple as 432.081hz?) You, just you right now at this moment (since you must be listening to the voice behind these words in a singular moment of time in your life, right?) can 'tap' into this inner life at any time…you just need to know 'how' to do it. Is there one method? NO…is there a one-size-fits-all methodology to this? NO…is this method that we're talking about on this YT channel and within this little book a method for YOU? Maybe? Maybe not…but here's the thing: you must try all these methods out for you and your own personal hero's journey. You must 'tune into the right frequency' for you and your journey, all the while awakening to the fact that this journey of awakening is just that: an awakening. What are you awakening to???

That is the question! What are you awakening to??? You're awakening to the reality that you have been asleep you're entire life, living as a robot amongst other robots living robotic lives fueled by the toxicity of other robots who have also been asleep…all the while thinking that you and all the other robots in the orbit of your life are awake and creating your own destiny with a ready supply of free will at your disposal...this awakening is the moment you realize you've been living in a dream world all this time as time seems to be slipping past you and you have been helpless to stop it...helpless until now.

You're discovering you must learn how to use your body like a spiritual antenna, taking good care of it, making sure its tuned into the right frequency (s) at the right time with meditation, cold showers or ice baths, proper nutrition with a concentration on keeping your Pineal Gland decalcified, and above all moderation in your sex life, eating, drinking and screen time, etc., etc., etc...You are an antenna which needs to be all about listening to these higher frequencies from these other worlds of true reality which have been swirling around you all this time that you've asleep in the belly of this white whale we call Earth.

# Chapter Three:
# The Gnostic failure and vital influence

## The Most Important Thing the Gnostics got Right

The Gnostics have fascinated me since I was 19 years old, and I discovered Elaine Pagels' seminal work called 'The Gnostic Gospels.' I wondered: why they were so oppressed? Why was their cosmology and their lifestyle and theology so violently persecuted as heretical? Why were these fellow Christians treated like evil serpents, chased into oblivion by the likes of St. Patrick and St. Irenaeus? What magical secrets did they hold within their nous, the rhythm of countless dives into the depths of the human psyche, reaching levels of consciousness no church politician could ever imagine reaching? Why were their clergy so virtuous and kind as they chose to live amongst the poor? Why were they so open to female spiritual leadership and wisdom? What was lost to us? What was lost?

What was lost to us as a species (or just our Western Civilization alone) when the Albigensian Crusade had not veered off course on the Feast Day of Mary Magdalene of July 22, 1209, and butchered the entire village of Beziers (population estimated at between 8,000-9,000) in Southern

France? It wasn't (according to Sean Martin in his book 'The Cathars: The Rise and Fall of the Great Heresy') directly due to heretical theology that they were slaughtered. Only indirectly. The problem was the Cathars weren't acknowledging the political power of the Catholic Church in Rome (which they labeled as the Church of Satan) as a tool of the Satanic Power which ruled this planet. These Gnostics would not bow down to the political power of the Catholic Church in Rome and for this they were slaughtered. Seven years earlier in 1202 the 4th Crusade began and by 1204 the Catholic-led crusade decided not to attack Muslims in the Holy Land, rather they veered toward their fellow Christians in Constantinople. Constantinople (present day Istanbul, Turkey) was the capitol of the drastically weakened Holy Roman Empire which had been at odds with the Church in Rome since the Great Schism in 1054 which officially established the Catholic Church as a direct political competitor with the Orthodox Church.

The slaughter in Beziers was no different: it was all about power and control. The Cathars weren't playing by the rules of the church, and they would pay dearly for it. Incidentally the church authorities were only looking for 222 Cathars in this town of 8-9k but the leadership of the town of Beziers would not give them up. Under the leadership of a notorious man named Arnold Amaury, the Crusaders gained entrance into the town and chaos and carnage ensued and he was asked what should be done to try and find these 222 Cathars and spare the rest of the town.  He uttered the command "Kill them all.  God will recognize his own."

## A Complicated Cosmology

The Gnostics had a tragically complicated cosmology. This complicated worldview would be their undoing.  But they were so 'right' in so many ways.  They had it right when they expressed a basic belief in the explanation of the Universe as a prison with the Earth as the oubliette or dungeon.  Our job is to find a master (let's say Jesus or John the Baptist for the Masons or the Rosicrucians or Cathars) who can help you escape from this horrific place we call home. This Master will assist you in finding your way out of the labyrinth of the underworld (like the caves of Moria beneath the Kingdom of Khazad-dum in the Lord of the Rings) as the knowledge that is contained within your sleepy mind is awakened.  This knowledge or 'gnosis' is within you and must be drawn out of you as you slowly awaken from this slumber.

The Gnostics had an extremely individualized view of this process of awakening.  There was no room for any of the trappings of the outward religious practices of the church with the club membership archetype of our modern, shallow Christianity here in the West. I still to this day identify deeply with Gnostics and their energy and enthusiasm for the individual path. This individualized nature of the process within Gnosticism is one of the major reasons for its demise but ironically it is also one of the reasons for this 'inner church' which we are speaking of here remained hidden or secret until people like Gurdjieff and Ouspensky and Mouravieff and Amis and Ashanin came along and uncovered it: namely the profound individual nature of the hero's journey. This journey is not completed by joining a church or agreeing with a certain doctrine. It takes a guide and a group and a developed astral body to guide you out the Oubliette...and a lot of luck from the other side...at least 'luck' is one word for it...but what are words, really?

A good summation of the very complicated cosmology of the Gnostics is found in a little book entitled "Religions of the Hellenistic-Roman Age" by Antonia Tripolitis. The Gnostics were very prominent within the 2nd and 3rd Century Christian community as it struggled and grew in spirit and number. The Neronian persecution began around 64 CE as Nero sought a scape goat for his fire and his mismanagement and ineptitude. Gnosticism began to mesh and mingle with Christianity (via teachers like Basilides, Valentinius and Marcion) as they were both an answer to the harsh, brutal physical, spiritual, emotional, and social suffering of this era.

Professor Tripolitis thinks that Christianity and Gnosticism merged in the 2nd and 3rd Centuries because of one event that did not happen: the *Parousia* or Christ's return. The early Christians were waiting and waiting for this return to sweep away all evil of this world but when it did not occur there were attempts to try and adjust to being stuck here in this world, continuing to wait upon the return of the promised cleansing of the evil, death, and destruction which this confusing world brings.

Gnosis offered a revealed knowledge or *gnosis* which was already contained within their psyche. This attainment of gnosis allowed that person to achieve salvation. The Gnostics rejected this prison life of an existence as the world was seen as a prison and the Earth its Oubliette or dungeon which we must escape from, using guides such as Jesus and John the Baptist to make our escape. We must learn through this gnosis *how* to return to our Maker, return to the Light of the Unknown Supreme God. This search for gnosis frees us from all worldly concerns with all its trivial legal, social, and moral rules and regulations. They were either aesthetic or libertine in their approach, the former removing himself or herself from the world like a monk, the latter rejecting the world by partaking in the excesses and lifestyle of the amoral, sexual, and social world, like a Jim Morrison from the Doors. The

Gnostics considered themselves an elite group as the 'spiritual members' of humanity. Only they were in on the fix and had the answer to true salvation. Everyone else was either a *pneumatikoi,* i.e. a spiritual being where the spark of the 'Unknown God' is predominate, a *psychikos,* i.e. someone who possesses a soul and free will but lacks gnostic enlightenment but is still capable of attaining a lower level of enlightenment and entrance back into the *Pleroma* which is the home of enlightened beings or *aeons,* or they were a *hylikos,* i.e. someone who is dominated by the carnal element and is spiritually ignorant with no sense of the need for salvation and thus no possibility of being saved.

Since the discovery of the Nag Hammadi Codices in 1945 there has been a resurgence in interest in Gnosticism, especially with Hans Jonas's seminal text entitled 'The Gnostic Religion' and Elaine Pagel's popular and beautifully written exploration. But we live in an age where the answers to all our ills are thought to be hidden from us therefore we see discoveries like the Gnostic texts at Nag Hammadi and the Essene texts of the Dead Sea Scrolls (both discovered curiously at the end of the Second World War) as proof that we need only these teachings in order for our religion to be made whole with the strength and grace and love which God intended…and in this case there is truth in this…let's talk…

The Gnostics gave certain people inclusion and security within their group, but they were made irrelevant by their amazingly complicated cosmology and an impersonal and arrogant way about their evangelism. They were divided among a myriad of different groups,  each led by a different guide who was an aesthetic or libertine with a different take on the path to salvation. They were so wildly complicated and exclusive that they were not able to give a complete and consistent '*how.*' In other words, although they were on the right track, they presented their search for an inner science in such a way as to exclude most seekers. Robin Amis speaks of this at length in the fifth chapter titled "Gnosis is not Gnosticism" from his book 'A Different Christianity' which was published in 1995. But Amis speaks compassionately on those who seek enlightenment through the Gnostics as the church and their blabbering, clownish clergy are unable to give an answer to the question of the existence of an inner church hence the hungry go to where the food is, although this spiritual food which the Gnostics offer is undercooked in a big way.

Amis says this,

'The essential difference between the Christian gnosis
and that of the Gnostics is in the quality of the
knowledge itself. In Christian esotericism, the true *faith*
taught by the gospel and the Fathers forms the basis,
the seed of a special kind of *inner knowledge;* it describes
an inner reality, known first in words, but finally at the
level of experience, as the Word, which cannot entirely
put into spoken words, and all of which, when put into
words, is liable to be misunderstood. It also includes
psychological teaching which relates to ways to obtain
the meaning of the teaching and put it into practice.
The reality expressed by these teachings is at core
*unchanging* and thus undifferentiated in the Platonic
sense. The theological disagreements that have
accumulated over two millennia are caused by
misunderstandings of language, by the Babel of
tongues.

Often it is possible to see that two sides in a
disagreement of doctrine are both motivated by the desire to
preserve the same inner truth. It is to avoid such
misunderstandings that esotericism took the form of an
"unwritten tradition," and it was almost certainly to avoid the
political disagreements that go with these understandings-
even today-that it has also sometimes been kept secret,

at least since the time of Clement's exile from Alexandria as a result of such misunderstandings.

God's providence and wisdom must be discerned through a method which rises above our normal human methods of knowledge and understanding. Language is ultimately unable to contain the meaning of God. You need to develop other-worldly means of communication beyond comprehension. The Spirit of the Risen God of the Desert must be perceived through other means, the intellect cannot discern it. The higher emotional center must be developed in such a way as to awaken the third eye, the Pineal Gland shaken of its calcified crust from this modern existence, and we must allow for the breath of God to enter the sanctuary of our mind, the womb of the nous where the infant is born again and again, anew each day with a new life each day. But this is not an easy task…it takes years of guidance and patience as the dark night of the soul awaits us. We must pass through a period of initiation which purifies us, prepares us and presents us as a worthy vessel to contain the secrets of God of the Universe as seen complete in the life eternal of the human known as Jesus of Nazareth. Amis writes this beautiful sentence toward the end of the chapter, 'As Saint Isaac the Syrian said, it is often only possible to perceive the providence of God when we possess no other support: when we have "no safety net" in our lives.'

The problem with the Gnostics to the leaders of the Early Church was this: they relied too heavily on the toxic imagination of too many who had not yet evolved, hence ideas which were not from the original source but from the source of a still fallen soul...THE fountain so to speak had not been reached by their spiritual guides. This is not to say that many of them had evolved and were indeed in touch with this source just as we are speaking of here, such as the writers of the Gospel of Mary Magdalene or the Gospel of Thomas. I find these and other select writings and companion pieces beautiful and connected to the source of Wisdom of the Gospels. But this is determined by my own discernment process and must also be determined by your discernment process.

True gnosis must remain pure and complete in its source and must be passed on from a person to another person...from a child of light to a child still in the darkness and this child in the darkness must be teachable, ready and willing to do whatever it takes to climb out of the Oubliette (a wonderfully true image which originated with the Gnostics). The true gnosis is beyond words, beyond the intellect and beyond a doctrine...it cannot be taught from a book or a traditional classroom...it must be awakened from within our nous, within our psyche so that it will not be forgotten like any other knowledge that is taught in school. This awakening occurs as if light is pulling light out of the darkness of the pit…this light that pulls must be pure with a power to attract that which cannot be seen to the visible and earthly eye…these masters of the light cannot be novices, they must be trained by the light itself, purified by the source of energy that can only arrive when it arrives, the grace of this awakening happens when it happens.

The Gnostics were too confusing with their focus on the imagination and the intellect being the main source of knowledge or gnosis…true gnosis is unspoken, clear and crisp and by its very nature unforgettable because it is already within us…it is remembered and it takes a certain type of human being to call this memory out of a darkened psyche…Charles Ashanin called these people 'spiritual mid-wives.'

It is spoken in a different language, a language only a certain developed organ within the psyche can understand and this organ must be awakened and nurtured and developed by a teacher and by a community of believers but most importantly by a human being who seeks to be more than a crawling creature scraping its claws on the ocean floor…it seeks to reclaim its inheritance as a child of Light, as a member of the Esoteric Circle.

The Gnostics were obviously on the right path with ample proof of their imagery and thought process.  For instance, their belief that the Universe is a prison, and the Earth its Oubliette is spot-on accurate. I find this true because it is my own experience of this place I live...it feels and has always felt like a prison to me, a place where I arrived a stranger and will leave a stranger...a place where I do not fit in, where the customs are strange and the people are strange and ever since I was a small child I have felt like I was always looking out for allies, looking out for my 'contacts' behind enemy lines...but it is the culture of this place which I love with art speaking to me stronger than anything else...the music I love, the authors I cherish, the paintings I connect with all speak to me of a different place, of a different time. I connect with art because they contain influences which are energy for me (Mouravieff calls them 'b' influences). Their origin is from another 'place' where space and time truly melt off the face of the clock and are irrelevant as ideas, drifting off like morning fog, revealing a new language of the mind where we are not dependent on these fragile bodies to do the work of 'hearing.' The inner heart hears with 'tongues in trees, books in running brooks, sermons in stones, and good in everything.' (*As You Like It,* Act 2, Scene 1). This development of a listening 'device' within us is the reason we are here on this planet, for those of us who are destined for the Esoteric Circle, that is. We of the Esoteric Circle are a different people from a different time and place and we are planning our return and seek others like ourselves to escape this Oubliette and make our way back…these who are my true kin…but it is not this place that I call home…these creatures are strange to me…they lurk about in the shadows of their minds, picking at bones and mucking about with the crawling creatures which take their nourishment from the waste of other crawling creatures…they are not my kin…The Gnostics knew about this aspect of reality and they were right…they were also correct as they knew that a guide is needed in order to lead us out of this nightmarish Oubliette as the Christian Gnostics like Valentinius recognized correctly that Jesus Christ was such a rare guide. But more specifically (and to the point of your spiritual journey) the Gnostics were correct in realizing that each of us need a personal guide to help assist us in our escape (whether it is through 7 levels or 12 levels) …we need a guide…you need a guide to help you escape from this strange and beautiful place we temporarily call home. We need to escape.

## Simulation Theory

We need to escape this place that is filled with dangers and perils which speak of not only the survival of humanity but also the survival of all of creation here on this little planet as we know it. This little planet we call home is a crucial gathering spot for angels and devils, being a location of great importance on the scale of creation. And if the Gnostics were correct and this planet is a simulated experiment by some extraterrestrial species (who they called 'Archons') just wanting to steal our vital energies (our 'soul' if you will) then our only hope is to purify our lower, animal multiplicity of 'selves' and develop true being, some sort of permanence, some degree of salvation before we leave this fallen place...this 'mixtus orbis.'

Our planet is a purification station of sorts, a place where souls are developed into spirits, gaining vital energies for the next layer of creation (which we humans cannot see through our five senses). In short, this planet is an essential source of energy for the world beyond this one, a place worth fighting for each individual cell at a time. You are a beautiful cell, a beautifully underdeveloped, un-activated and unusual cell in the body of God. You are not just a downloadable bundle of information we call 'consciousness' which can be shot by a laser beam to any distant star or spaceship or planet, making the body a thing of the past. You are more, much more than information. The brain is not just a 'computer' that is programmable with a set operating system with a binary coded language discernable to all other makes and models...You are a porthole to another reality and this planet is where you purify...this is where you spiritually de-tox.

Think of yourself as a cell within the mind of God. Your general cosmic job during this short span of linear time here on this planet is to grow this cell into a healthy, functioning part of the mind of God, developing it and being a part of creation itself. To be this healthy cell, you must have a quality about you, we'll call that the quality of permanence. This is what you're working towards: a state of permanence.

The Simulation Theory has fascinating Gnostic overtones. Is this world just a computer simulation we cannot escape from, no matter what we do? And if it is a simulation then are their certain methods which we can utilize to break free from this matrix? Is this what all of us are after, those of us who are interested in the Esoteric (whether it be satanic, magic, Christian, Gnostic, or whatever angle)? Are we just looking to break through to the other side via spells or rituals or frequencies or liturgies or ice baths or crystals or mushrooms or DMT or pot or meth or booze or sexual ritual and sacrifice. Aren't we just looking for a hack to escape this place?

# Chapter Four:
# Alexander the Great and the age of anxiety

## Alexander the Great and the Importance of Hellenization

This unwritten teaching has been literally passed down to us through the Apostles. It is as precious as gold, a valuable to us as breath and is the energy which encompasses our psyche as God passes through us, reviving us and making us whole and radiant and evolved. Our birthright is quite literally our second birth.

Remember: truth leads to understanding, not confusion.

Why were there so many seekers in the days of Christ? I mean not only did Christianity and Gnosticism arise from this era, but also the mystery cults like Mithraism became popular, alongside the religious philosophies for the well-educated minorities and Hellenistic Judaism as the Pentateuch and Hebrew Scriptures were translated into Greek (called the Septuagint) allowed Judaism to finally become a world religion. This question and the comparison with our day is worth a closer look.

It all goes back to the Hellenization (331 BCE-31 BCE) of the Mediterranean by a very Oedipal Alexander the Great who took over where his father Phillip II failed, namely, to conquer the Persian Empire and expand the Roman Empire.  Expand it Alexander did, and in short order as well starting with the defeat of the Persian King Darius III at the battle of Gangamela in 331.  By the time of Alexander's untimely death in 323 he had created the Roman Empire which stretched from the Aegean Sea to the Indus River in India and from the Black Sea to the north to the Sahara in north Africa.  This conquest was driven by many things (political and military power, personal glory and the Oedipal conquering of his father) but to our point, his conquest enabled the culture of the Romans to spread far and wide with its technology, politics, social, religious and educational systems now being exported along with their iron grip on those they conquered (and I mean 'iron'…they were absolutely brutal).  This spreading of the Roman Empire and their culture was establishing what they called *oikoumene* or a common, close-knit, self-contained culture united by their Greek culture and language.  The Romans had an amazing aspect of their culture which others do not (but our 'Western' culture *does* have), namely that of *adaptability.* The Greeks had the ability to adapt a new culture and a new geography and a new geo-political environment while still maintaining the strength of their oikoumene.  One of the key aspects of this entire expansion of Greek culture was one subtle feature which impacted the expansion of Christianity: the technological development and replication of roads. The Greeks built roads and allowed people to begin to travel like never before. This allowed for people to begin to mix with other people, exposing them to new customs, new products, new food, new gods and new ways to see reality. This development of the system of roads is the most important aspect of oikoumene because without it Christianity does not expand like it did in the first 300 hundred years after Christ. Without the Greeks and Hellenization, Christianity does not flourish and expand and reach the ends of the Earth. But with this expansion of the Greek culture their came a cost.

This phase of the expansion of Greek culture by the Romans allowed their influence to irreversibly alter the socio-economic, political, and religious world in every place they conquered or bordered. It unified these conquered cultures in what Tripolitis calls *syncretism*. It took the provincial and made it universal. It took the collective and made it individual. The next phase after Hellinization ended in 31 This defeat ushered in a new age of insecurity and anxiety due to this literal mixing up and meshing of different cultures and religions and customs. This is the Hellenistic-Roman Age (30 BCE when Antony and Cleopatra were defeated at Actium.

(BCE- 4th Century CE). Notice how this matches our age of tumult...the old rules did not apply any longer, the rules of society and culture and religion melted away as people became more mobile and individualistic. The old ways began to break down and nothing was certain as people were free to move about and explore and decide what they wanted to do instead of what their provincial life and family structure decided for them. Now they no longer had a hand-me-down god...they need a personal god who understood their struggle to become something different than their social structure dictated. The Greeks brought freedom and choice and liberty...what a new burden all these choices, right?

With so much uncertainty people began to search for certainty, into the next life...they sought *soteria* or salvation to give them release from this uncertainty and the misery of hand-to-mouth, daily life. They were looking for a savior, a personal savior and they began to search for these answers in the mystery cults, philosophy, Christianity, Gnosticism, and Judaism. Within this grand cultural experiment which Alexander unknowingly began, the different religions and their gods began to travel these new Roman roads. Along their way they began to adapt and change with the different previously isolated societies, many of them of them were based on agricultural cults which celebrated the drama of the seasons. When you take an agricultural cult and remove it from the land itself you need a home where the seeds can be planted and germinate. That new land was the psyche or soul/spirit of the human being itself. Everyone's mind or psyche (nous) was the 'land' itself with a savior sought after to bring deliverance and protection to the individual who sought a guide to the promised land of the soul. Christianity is literally a result of this inward movement of an agricultural cult combined with the mystical teaching of an enlightened human being named Jesus Christ. It is this commixture which we experience as Christianity, and it is this individualistic nature of it which allowed it to be so attractive to the people of the Hellenistic-Roman period.

### Jesus and mirror of our time

One thing that is absolutely for sure: this planet we inhabit is a chaotic blend of good and evil and the goal (I suppose) is to tune into the Goodness and make your great escape to the world that is awaiting you on the other side…but let's talk about the evil side of this world…it's so evil that words have not been invented to describe the sinister aspect of what this truly means. We are so caught up in the business of sleep and staying asleep that we can barely stomach the truth of how evil this is…Dostoevsky said it best when he describes in his novels the two aspects of Satan as

Lucifer as the energy that haunts us trying to isolate us and then of course there is Ahriman whose energy seeks to annihilate us and destroy any trace of us. There is an element within the framework of these two energies which supports the creation of fear upon this planet, which feeds off this fear and anyone who feels it, allowing it to flow through their mind, filling the ruts of thoughts which have been plowed and plowed deeply within their psyche so that nothing else flows there but fear and the love of fear and need to keep it flowing through these ruts, these beds like a river flowing to the lowest level of your being where all your energy is enslaved to the darkest and deepest parts of your being, the place where the worms and the stench and the magots and filth mingle, suffocating all your light that you have inherited (long before your birth). This planet of ours is a fear factory. Until you suffer enough and grow tired of this enslavement you will continue to put up with it, happily and contentedly wallowing around with these bottom-feeders that you have convinced yourself that you are a part of, that you a member of…that you are a part of this species. But ahh, you are not a part of *this species*…you are different, aren't you and you've always known it, you've always felt out of place in world…as if you don't belong, you don't fit in…you don't remember these creatures…why?…because you are *not* a bottom-dweller…you are a child of light, one called back by your origin, back to your place of origin my friend…you are a child of light which seeks to escape the hell hole that is this Earth…you are a child of light and never ever forget this…you are a child of light. Here are the Scriptural testimonies…

Just as Christ says in **John 9:5** that "As long as I am in the world, I am the light of the world," he is transformed into light at the transfiguration. **Luke** writes in **16:8**, "And he was transfigured before them, and his face shone like the sun, and his clothes became white as light." St. Paul confesses to the presence of the light when he writes in **Ephesians 5:8**, "For at one time you were darkness, but now you are light in the Lord. Walk as children of light." And, from Paul in **1 Thessalonians 5:5**, "For you are children of light, children of the day. We are not of the night or of the darkness." Peter confesses likewise in **1 Peter 2:9**, "But you are a chosen race, a royal priesthood, a holy nation, a people for his own possession, that you may proclaim the excellencies of him who called you out of darkness into his marvelous light." This is the Scriptural witness to the existence of the Esoteric Circle.

Such weight brings tremendous responsibility, like a Shepherd for his Sheep: loyal, recklessly loyal, and true, to the death the Shepherd is loyal to his sheep…but the Shepherd is loyal to the lost sheep. It is in that loyalty that the secret of the Esoteric Brotherhood is found. Reckless loyalty.

**John Dominic Crossan and the human Jesus**

One of the most creative and controversial writers which the Western Christian church has produced in the 20th Century is John Dominic Crossan.  He's an Irish-born American scholar teaching out of DePaul University in Chicago, Illinois.  His controversial book entitled "Jesus: A Revolutionary Biography" is a grandiose title which lives up to its name…it is a compassionate and beautifully written and immaculately researched work which does something unique: it balances the miraculous, mystical side of Jesus with the social-justice warrior Jesus.  In short it satisfies (as far as I am concerned) both the Western and the Eastern fascinations with the spiritual and the human Jesus, both of which are out of balance.  Indeed, Crossan gives us a balance of both the human and the spiritual side of Jesus, this book I believe is the highest achievement of his amazing academic career.

In chapter 3 Crossan speaks of this concept of 'open commensality' within the ministry of Jesus.  The term 'commensality' is defined as the rules of tabling and eating as miniature models for the rules of association and socialization. The root word within commensality is the Latin 'mensa' meaning 'table.'  It must be properly understood how aggravating Jesus was to the established religious order of his day, i.e. the Pharisees and Sadducees. Let's look in detail at a passage from Eugene H. Peterson's interpretation in 'The Message' where in Luke 14: 21-26 this story speaks quite plainly about the intentions of Jesus's ministry;

"That triggered a response from one of the guests: "How fortunate the one who gets to eat dinner in God's kingdom." Jesus followed up, "Yes. For there was once a man who threw a great dinner party and invited many. When it was time for dinner, he sent out his servant to the invited guests, saying, 'Come on in; the food's on the table.'

"Then they all began to beg off, one after another making excuses. The first said, 'I bought a piece of property and need to look it over. Send my regrets.'

"Another said, 'I just bought five teams of oxen, and I really need to check them out. Send my regrets.'

"And yet another said, 'I just got married and need to get home to my wife.'

"The servant went back and told the master what had happened. He was quickly outraged and told the servant, 'Quickly, get out into the city streets and alleys. Collect all who look like they need a square meal, all the misfits and homeless and wretched you can lay your hands on, and bring them here.'

"The servant reported back, 'Master, I did what you commanded-and there's still room.'

"The master said, 'Then go to the country roads. Whoever you find, drag them in. I want my house full! Let me tell you, not one of those originally invited is going to get so much as a bite at my dinner party.'"

Amazing story from Luke...says it all really. Crossan continues this thought process (some rare ideas are storehouses of fine spiritual energies) with this question: what happens to social order when everyone is invited to the 'table' and they 'sit' together and eat next to one another? In the time of Jesus eating was such a social statement, what you ate, who you ate with, where you sat with those you ate with, on and on...Jesus basically says, how about we just eat together without using the socio-political-tribal map? Well...this not only disrupted the social and religious and economic order of the day it downright threatened it, but therefore Jesus was also labeled a glutton and a drunkard and eventually murdered for this threat. Because you see, Jesus was a genius (even though Crossan makes the claim that Jesus was almost assuredly illiterate since he would have had no access to education being in the lowest 15% of the poorest of the poor class as a lowly 'carpenter') with not only high intelligence but also high emotional intelligence. He was a talker, straight to the face of the authorities but, but he could also back it up and think and talk circles around his opponents.

Jesus was o.k. with exchanging his honor for the Kingdom. So Crossan makes this point that an illiterate peasant from Palestine had a dream of a just and equal Kingdom here on this Planet, in the here and now regardless of what race a person was born into, regardless of what class a person was born into or regardless of what religion someone was born into...the Kingdom is meant for anyone who has 'ears to hear.'

The 'church' then was just like the 'church' is today: arrogant, prejudiced, power-hungry and pathetic, only focused on maintaining its own socio-economic and political place in society (regardless of how many pedophiles and sex-offending narcissists are hiding amongst their clergy rank and file). Jesus attempted to pull the spiritual out of the 'church' while maintaining His connection with the harsh reality of human existence here on this planet. Jesus was after all born in a manger which symbolizes the birth of the 'nous' within the flesh of our human body. If we don't have a balance, then we are lost. (this is, a main reason the Gnostics were not successful: they were either aesthetics via abstinence from worldly pleasure or libertine via excess, they had not *balance* between the two).

Crossan does an amazing job at revealing a balance within the character of Jesus Christ, one which is desperately needed as Christianity is at a turning point in this age of Artificial Intelligence. We need a fully divine and a fully human Jesus Christ, otherwise the Esoteric teaching is 'missing the mark' and ceases to be by definition "esoteric.' It becomes 'law.' The definition of the word 'sin' is to "miss the mark."

### Shepherd of the Flock

What is it which will bring us back from our wandering? To sit in the stillness of the morning and remember that small voice echoing in the sanctuary of our mind, hearing Shakespeare whisper "tongues in trees, books in brooks, sermons in stones and good in everything" and realizing that the sweet voice of the Good Shepherd calling us back to the flock, saying in a whisper, "I am the good shepherd...the good shepherd lays down his life for the sheep...I am the good shepherd" and "I know my own my own know me."

The good shepherd has compassion for his flock, just as **Matthew** wrote in **9:36** recording, "When he saw the crowds, he had compassion for them, because they were harassed and helpless, like sheep without a shepherd."

It is without question that a chief characteristic of a member of the Esoteric Circle is a reckless loyalty to those who are 'harassed and helpless.' For in lending aid to such a situation, the creature within us is minimized and we are elevated, both sheep and Shepherd rise above the clicking and crawling condition of our Earthly birth. Implicit within this idea of the reckless loyalty of the Shepherd is the presence of sacrifice and suffering for the sake of the helpless and harassed sheep.

# Chapter Five:
# Surviving [American] Christianity

Are you a survivor of American Christianity? Welcome my friend, let's talk a bit about this...I guess we should begin with the definition of a survivor, right? By 'survivor' I mean you have been a church goer, member and participant in some way or another during your lifetime. Maybe you were baptized as an infant or in youth group or as an adult...maybe you went through Confirmation Class and became an official member of a specific church...maybe you struggled fitting into a youth group or a Sunday School class, you know, the church was a place of socialization for you, it was your social connection with friends and family. But maybe, just maybe something happened to you...an awakening if you will...a spiritual awakening. But here's the rub: there was no one to talk to about *what* had happened to you...there was no one around to explain what had happened and what to do next? And when you did try and talk to someone it seemed to lead nowhere...or worse yet it brought out the narcissists in your orbit, attracting some of the church leadership (possibly your pastor or youth pastor) who were just a low-level bureaucrat, over-achieving idiots or God-forbid, predators (whether they be emotional or sexual predators) and abusing narcissists.

Not only did you make it to your spiritual awakening through the myriad of obstacles within a church-setting, but you remained hungry for more. You knew there was something more, didn't you? There was something within you that remembered there was a different way, a deeper way, knew there was more to life than this toleration…the way of this world is always whispering to you: tolerate. You got a taste of true freedom and now you want more…you awakened but you need a spiritual guide to help you navigate through the purification stage. Yes…congratulations…you survived American Christianity…now what?

**How to Tune Your Self**

Let's talk again about this idea of the antenna (ideas are really 'arks' which carry the fantastic creatures of another land, salvaged from some distant cataclysm…ideas are alive and organic beings which float about the Universe waiting to be plucked up out of the ocean of creation, like some water-logged sailor bobbing up and down on the surface after a great while whale struck his boat and swallowed his mates…ideas are alive)…In order to capture these ideas you really need to learn how to tune yourself. How to tune yourself…let's talk about that for a bit…you can tap into this inner life. Christ speaks of this constantly when he says repeatedly 'for those who have to hear.' What does that mean? You must know this…what does it mean?

You are an antenna, a spiritual antenna that needs to be tuned to the correct frequency. You are receiving messages constantly from the other side but you cannot hear them…and all the while your time here in the Oubliette is moving forward like a movie that you can't stop and before you know it your time for retirement is upon you and all the kids are gone you look at your hands and there's nothing but sand slipping through your bony little fingers…how does this happen? The reason is (quickly): you are out of tune with the Universe. You are miserably out of tune, and you cannot hear anything that is happening outside your puny five senses.

It is amazing that Marvel and DC and George Lucas and JRR Tolkien are the prophets of our day when they tap into this concept of latent energy and the evolution of these inner capabilities. Nietzsche got it right and Gurdjieff and PD Ouspensky and Joseph Campbell expressed it: we all carry the potential to be 'Overman' or '*Ubermensch*' when he says in *Thus spoke Zarathustra,* 'I teach you the overman. Man is something that shall be overcome. What have you done to overcome him? All beings so far have created something beyond themselves; and you do not want to be the ebb of this great flood and even go back to the beasts rather than overcome man? What is the ape to man? A laughingstock or a painful embarrassment. And man shall be just that for the overman: a laughingstock or a painful embarrassment.

Behold I teach you the overman. The overman is the meaning of the earth […] Man is a rope, tied between beast and overman-a rope over an abyss…What is great in man is that he is a bridge and not an end: what can be loved in man is that he is an *overture* and a *going under*…'

This is the famous 'God is dead' passage which Conservative Christians love to quote here in the rusted and pitiful Bible belt of America, but they miss the obvious point: to truly discover this 'God' of ours you must let your old image die and allow a re-birth to occur within your psyche. You must have your own experiences of a Bethlehem and your own Jordan River and your own transfiguration and your own temptation in the desert and your own Golgotha and your own resurrection to truly be a Christian. This is the meaning of that passage by Nietzsche, not the death of our religion by some evil pagan philosopher.

The real culprit lies from the death within the soul of American Christianity. In 2024 Americans are leaving the church in droves not because of politics and the immorality of the far right or the far left. Americans are leaving the church because it has no path toward a deep experience of the Holy…it has no spirituality. It only offers religion with its rules and creeds and organizational structure.

Plain and simple: the American church in 2024 is a two-dimensional, political club that has lost touch with its cosmic roots. American Christianity is dying because it has no directions to the Inner Life. It has lost contact with the teaching which leads to everlasting life...the true deep waters which Christ Jesus speaks of...it has lost touch with its heart. It needs people to find their 'inner church.' It needs a group of pastors who are Shamans instead of warmed-over car and insurance salesmen and wannabe politicians. The church needs to encourage its clergy to go on the hero's journey and then welcome these Shaman back into the tribe...but alas, those days are long gone. The Shaman who leaves the tribe and goes on this epic hero's journey will return to the village only to find it abandoned, the place burned to the ground. As Christ says in **Matthew 8:20**, "Foxes have holes and birds of the air have nests, but the Son of Man has no place to lay his head."

Our call to the Overman is not a call to look at the color of one's skin in order to find purity. This purity of the Overman is made, not born. The seed is discovered and then germinated and cultured and protected and watered until it has gone to seed itself. This is the truth. Members of the Esoteric Circle are made not born in perfect condition as automatic members of this church or this 'race' or this country or this place. It is a process of purification which implies sacrifice and pain and struggle.

This is the message of the Early Church and the

message which Robin Amis speaks of in his seminal work on this lost Christianity in his 1995 publication *A Different Christianity.* Saints are made, not born…in other words we must work diligently while it is day light to rise out of our beast-like nature. As Charles Ashanin told me, 'Without higher consciousness we are just crawling creatures.' We must work at this unburdening our psyches of our karmic burden and well as all the genetically inherited garbage we have inherited from our ancestors. It takes a lifetime to accomplish this with only a few dozen years to truly make headway in this unburdening. Soon the lights begin to fade in this mind and there will no longer be the advantage of willpower which you need to sustain this unburdening. You must work while it is daylight to be counted as a member of this Esoteric Circle, this cosmic family of higher consciousness.

The energy and inspiration behind this collapse is not a new religion, but rather no religion at all. People aren't leaving the church for another choice. Their choice is nothing at all. People are just leaving. But if you want to put a label on which religion is winning the hearts and minds of a new generation of spiritually hungry Americans and Europeans that would be Luciferianism. Just take a look at movies and music and cartoons in 2024…I mean open your eyes and see the images that are flashed before you…movies like Ari

Aster's 2019 *Midsommer*, Alex Hirsch's cartoon from 2012 called *Gravity Falls*, Sam Smith's 2023 Grammy performance of '*Unholy*'...these are massively heretical against a Christianity that literally has no one to defend her...I found all of these absolutely repulsive to watch and a sad symptom that the battle may already be lost, a call to the Esoteric Circle to gather up and preserve the wisdom for the coming storm...

...whether we like it or not *homo sapiens* must worship something. Since there is no inner church and no Esoteric Circle to help guide and sustain the spiritual equilibrium of a culture then that religion will die and the chaos and the anarchy which infiltrated that religion will prevail and humanity will have to wallow about in the muck as its proud technological achievements and marvels have their way with their own creator and the human experiment will cease, only to be merged and folded into the churning rotation of creation itself (the whimper of its presence from our *Anthropocene* epoch which officially began in 1955 with the steady presence of *plutonium-239*)...unless the Esoteric Circle is revived.

### Survivors of a Sick Church

We who are called out into this world (which is Ted Nottingham's definition of the church: a gathering of those who are called out) must band together in a tight knit group, gather up the energy that is surging around this planet at such a time as this and evolve…we must evolve into our roles as vital members of this Esoteric Circle, otherwise our species is doomed and this experiment is over.  Remember this: the Earth is a test-lab so to speak.  We must not allow our generation to be the generation which allowed the circle to break.

Let me talk a little about the church, because some of you are survivors of some horrific experiences (physical, sexual, and spiritual) within a church setting, particularly those of you who have experienced sexual abuse by a priest or pastor or youth pastor or deacon or elder or whomever. You've been abused and yet you have survived.  You are broken and abused yet still have this spark of Christ within you…what are you supposed to do?  Just because you've been hurt doesn't mean you're done being a seeker, right?  Just because someone took advantage of your age, your immaturity, your addiction, your disease, your innocence doesn't mean you are now ineligible to continue your spiritual journey.  You have every right to be made whole again…you are a good person, a loving person and an equal to anyone sitting in those pews and what was done to you was evil, sinful and awful…but here you are, still alive and the person who did this to you is still haunting your dreams, still mocking you as the closing your sleepy eyes…remember that Christ came to this Planet to speak to us…he came to speak to us so that we may be made *whole* again.  There is nothing that has ever happened to you (no matter how awful and sinister, mean, and destructive, abusive, and tortuous) that cannot be healed.  God can heal this brokenness which has ruled your life.

## A Prayer for the Broken

…you are a good person loved by God, the Maker of heaven and earth and you are worthy of this healing which you seek…claim it and work toward it and then wait for the grace of the Living Light to awaken within your sleepy soul, pulling all your tiny selves together, binding together their memories of the distant wicked past and your painful present and bringing you wholeness, harmony and radiance within the eye of your beautiful and unified 'I' having been healed of your past and now set on solid ground to stay a little while longer on this Earth so you can be a healed and whole cell within the body of the living Creator and no longer thrown into the trash heap of rotting memory and nasty Karma which stinks of the sweetness of dark death itself, where teeth are constantly gnashing by your ears, keeping you from any rest…now you can rest my friend, knowing that there is hope within the heart of Christianity and its name is Christ.  He will lead you out of this Oubliette, this dungeon, this pit in the center of the Castle we call Earth…Christ will be awakened within you and will lead you out…just claim it, work, and wait upon this Spirit of Spirits which commands this darkness to be gone and is the source of this light which is already within you.

# Chapter 6:

# How Does a Civilization lose its way?

## Of Shamans & Schizophrenics

This is difficult to hear as we in the West look upon psychological instability as a disease, one which is a pathological scourge which needs to be tamed by the psychopharmacological miracles of anti-psychotic medications distributed by well-meaning psychiatrists of every shape and form. But the ancient shaman cultures are well-established in their support of this demonized condition of the Saints, seeing a schizophrenic as a potential link with the other world, as a spiritual blessing, a long-lost diamond of sorts to their tribe. Our civilization sees the Schizophrenic as a dangerous, sick child of a long lost, barbarous age, as if their mind was a deformed limb that we just can't quite cut off. So many mentally ill fall prey to drug use as a form of self-treatment. So the ones who physically survive meth, alcohol or fentanyl are locked up in jails and prisons where they are subjected to violence and abuse and neglect or for the lucky ones they are sent off to actual psychiatric units and hospitals where they are sedated into submission. No matter how you look at it, our present civilization has no idea how to treat the mentally ill without abusing them in some form or another.

---

One of the signs of our decadence and spiritual decay as a Civilization is how we treat the mentally ill. We treat them as the sick ones, the criminally minded and insane who need to be abused, locked up and sedated for their own good, for the sake of society and its contents…for the safety of us all. I am not proposing that all schizophrenics need to be released immediately so that the Spirit of the One True God can be released upon this lowly planet. But I do want to ask a question. In treating the mentally ill as isolated anomalies that modern medicine needs to sedate and control and babysit until their bodies finally wear out their sick minds, maybe, just maybe are we muting voices which we need to hear, voices from the beyond which have been speaking to us all these many years? Maybe we, *we* sane ones are the sick ones in thinking we know how best to weed God's Garden…maybe we are the sick ones by thinking that we know best how to navigate the journey of our species. Just think though: our species has been around 900,000 years or so and only recently in the past 75 years begun to treat the mentally ill via sedation and quasi-incarceration, yet the previous approximately 899,925 years have told a different story, a very different story in how the mentally ill are deeply connected to the Universal Spirit we call God.

I'm interested in this idea: are a tiny percentage of the mentally ill hidden prophets? Are they the ones who are diving deeply into their subconsciousness, re-establishing the link with God and trying to guide us onto a healthy future as a species? You see, these are the kinds of questions the 'church' and theologians aren't asking…but they should be. Is our civilization sitting on a psychic gold mind and just don't know it? Is our civilization passing up on its opportunity to save itself from within its own dead and decaying psychic body? Or do we know it but just don't care…but we care more about letting the industry of modern medicine (i.e. the American Medical Association and the Sackler Brothers and Perdue Pharma) and our true religion of Capitalism to steer us into deep waters of the soul. Our civilization (which is quickly becoming one world civilization) has no spiritual leaders so it's quite convenient to disregard the mentally ill with apathy and disdain and let them fall into homelessness and drug and alcohol addiction, leaving the bulk of the responsibility of their care to be left to local law enforcement and the criminal justice system. I think this issue is enormously relevant to our spiritual crisis.

Because we rely on our economic philosophy to guide our sense of well-being and stability we are spiritually led astray, blindly following perverted and godless people like Elon Musk and Warren Buffett and the late Jeffrey Epstein to give us guidance, falsely believing that economic success is a sign of God's love and approval.

We are being led by con men disguising themselves as businessmen and politicians and sexual perverts disguising themselves as wise men, priests and ministers who are simply pawns of a Capitalist system which is overseeing the ecological destruction and taming of our planet who are leading us down a path of isolation and annihilation. We're over deep waters and now we discover that no one knows how to swim anymore. Our dying civilization is being guided by idiots and we just don't seem to care. We've destroyed all our teachers who can teach us how to 'swim' in the spiritual sense. Our world is burning, and we just let our iTunes algorithm choose for us. We just drown out the sound of the world burning. No more shamans. No more God. The pain and suffering, the burning and flooding is our Karma, and it must all be processed through our collective psychic body of humanity. Death will follow and new life will sprout from the ashen forest floor as the rain clouds finally build up above our sunken chests and drowsy eyes. We need new shamans.

Our civilization is missing a golden opportunity to see if our mentally ill are really a cosmic link into our collective future. As it is our global, money-worshipping civilization is accumulating horrific karma as we suppress the very voice of God within our midst.

Let's start over…

# How does a civilization lose its way?

It's crazy to think how cyclic our time is here on this spinning ball (we're spinning 1037 mph if you're at the equator and if you move halfway up the globe your speed slows to 733 mph). Comforting. Terrifying. Fascinating all at the same time…According to Dr. Greg Little the Americas were 'discovered' by Columbus in 1492 and a by the mid 1540's Hernando de Soto was exploring the land we know today as the Southern United States of Florida, Georgia, Mississippi, Arkansas  and north into the Mississippi River valley where he met his death in 1542 and unceremoniously dumped into that pristine river that now snakes polluted, plastic laden water into the Gulf of Mexico. At the time there was an estimated 57 million Native Americans living in the Americas with thousands of amazingly advanced and sophisticated cultures creating an intricate tapestry of 'savages' who would within a very short generation be reduced to a mere 5 million people as the introduction of diseases (in particular Smallpox) quickly decimated the population and crushed their entire civilization. A sort of collective amnesia took place as this civilization which was based on oral tradition lost its voice as the spiritual reservoir

of cosmic wisdom was dumped into the proverbial
Mississippi along with de Soto's body and the psychic fuel
which supplied the Spirit of space and time was snuffed out,
all in the literal pursuit of gold and slaves and land. The
giants who led these cultures (which were well-documented
by de Soto and his amazingly abusive and violent band of
Conquistadors) were said to tower above the rest, reportedly
7-8 feet in height (yet modern-day anthropologists explain
away this gigantic stature saying it was just their massive hair
which gave them the impression of a great height)…no matter
what their vast advantage in numbers and strength of will
were no match for an epidemic which tore through this
culture and left the massive serpents mounds in Missouri and
Illinois and Indiana to become overgrown with Cottonwood
and Cottonmouths as the songs which contained their heritage
soon became a whimper in the hollow mouth of time…Jared
Diamon in his bestseller entitled 'Guns, Germs, and Steel'
even states the same (although smaller numbers than Greg
Little) point as states the importance of disease and microbes
from the Europeans being the main culprits in the decimation
of these magnificent civilizations of the Americas as the
Spanish began leading the way for European colonization. Dr.
Diamond estimates that the decline in the population of the
natives within a generation of the 'discovery' by the mighty
and courageous Christopher Columbus was an astounding

95%...collective amnesia immediately took hold as their 'Esoteric Circle' was shattered, never to be healed, never to be made whole again…

…what would it take for our civilization to experience a similar fate?

### Life in the Retirement Home

…we live on this organism we call a planet as self-serving, toxic crawling creatures who never stop scraping our knuckles on the Ocean floor unless…unless we awaken to our divine birthright, this calling to advance past that pit we always seem to fall into, to leap the chasm and escape out of this repeated loop of lives, this churning over and over of sleep-drenched existence where life just seems to magically pass you by (again) you end up (if you're one of the socio-economically lucky) sitting in your new room at the retirement home where you have been abandoned by your loving children with a few sturdy Jack Daniels Whiskey boxes to unpack containing the curled and unlabeled pictures and souvenirs and bits of proof that you and your life really existed on the planet…but it all went so fast, this life…it really just passed me by…again…and you sit and wait for breakfast…then lunch…then you wait for 7:30 so you can go to bed…you're so tired…you just want to go to sleep in your new room, listening to the tick of the Timex watch you were given at your retirement party on that Friday afternoon so long ago…and you drift into thought as the illusion caresses your mind like candle smoke in a pitch-black room.

…we live in a civilization where we are constantly distracted and entertained and drugged in order to stay in line, stay groggy, stay luke-warm…we 'masses' are efficiently entertained so as not to ask too many question about the meaning of it all, the meaning of life and how to live it that we forget who we are in the cosmic sense of the word and we barely pick up a finger to do the work…oh sure there are moments of clarity when that little antenna called the Pineal Gland is momentarily activated when you're inundated with a bunch of b influences at a music concert or when you see some work of art which suddenly strikes you with its communication without comprehension or when you just stop in your tracks on an ordinary day and you look around you and everything looks familiar and new at the same time and you are content with the moment…but these moments are fleeting and you are quickly distracted back into slumber as the sounds of this grand circus seep back into our manger minds and we forget we had those moments, we forget that we carry the Logos of the Creator God and…we go back to sleep…because we are programmed creatures, like little silly computers who constantly live in the past, dragging memories into the present and poisoning our future. We need to find methods of re-programming our minds so that we can hear the voice of God in the clamor of our disintegration.

...to find evidence of this look no further than the level of money some human beings receive to constantly distract us: sports athletes and technology executives...sports and social media are such a tool of the General Law, it's amazing how obvious this is...remember this: to understand the moral composition of a people look at who they pay the most. This may sound simple, but it is a barometer of sorts, a gauge to see what a collective group truly and deeply values. The morally shallow spiritually decayed West values people who show no mercy to the Earth on their path to attaining power over nature, ruthless power over everything that falls underneath the grand umbrella of nature: climate, animal and insect, flora, fauna and 8 billion somnambulists all contained in a tiny little 200-hundred-mile-deep pocket of air wrapped around a planet orbiting an ordinary sun in the frozen vastness of an ever-expanding Universe. How difficult it is for even a tiny group of these sleepwalkers to realize the presence of that hidden gem which is contained within their groggy and delicate grey matter, that Logos, the seed of God within us that needs to be awakened and returned the body cosmos which calls and beckons us homeward. But until we awaken, we are just tiny crawling creatures looking for our next meal, being guided around by the nose, the chain being mistaken for God.

...you've asked this question for a long time, haven't you? What is the point?! Why am I here? There's just so much Schopenhauer and Nietzsche and Camus that you can read at the coffee house on a Fall morning on your day off that can fill this void that you're feeling...there's just so much Nirvana and Husker Du and Neil Young you can listen to that makes you feel like you've broken through to the other side like Huxley and Blake and Jim Morrison say...there's just so much poetry and paint and music that you can explore and produce and painstakingly nurture before you ask that magical question: what about me? What about my own expression of this passion, of this angst, this desire to be born again as Christ says...but Christ? What about me? Are these saints and artists just there to make me feel that I'm growing and evolving and awakening or am I finally ready to awaken on my own (without the constraints of a desire to be famous, rich, and admired for being a holy and blood-soaked genius who died on the Capitalistic altar of fame and fortune? What about me? Well...*what* about you? When IS it going to be your time to awaken?

Our main interest is this: how will the Esoteric Circle remain unbroken? How? But more importantly, the question is are *you* ready to stand in this Esoteric Circle as the world burns and drowns at the same time? Are you ready to be among the ones who will preserve this ancient wisdom for the next generation so that humanity can rebuild itself, learning again how to co-exist with the natural world as well as the holy presence of God within our collective psyches? We must evolve, but first we must survive. Are you willing to be a part of this secret school?

## Save the Planet by Awakening

Let me address any doubts you might have regarding your spiritual awakening: if you truly, earnestly are concerned about the collapse of our civilization (because that is what we're witnessing to the rise of populist tyrants to the collapse of weather patterns and ocean currents to the demise of religion through the growth of Artificial Intelligence) the best thing you can do is *spiritually awaken* and become a healthy, conscious cell in this sickly body of a planet…we need conscious people being awakened to their purpose in this world…God needs you awake, first and foremost…your spiritual awakening matters to the world…going 'inward' at a time like this…diving deeply as Melville did, into the unconscious deep waters of the soul to find that white whale and confront it...embracing it or being annihilated by it, there are only two choices...this going inward is a salvific act for the life you see around you, this life that is disintegrating all around you...it's like this: by going *inward* you heal the *outer.*

Just think of this: if dozens or a hundred or a thousand of us *homo sapiens* would awaken, right now while the planet is burning and drowning at the same cruelly ironic moment...what if we all awakened now?  What kind of fine energies would that bring to our planet?  What kind of beautifully ancient bell would be rung in the palace of the sun, signaling to God herself that the time has come to make a visit to this cold dark planet (as Gurdjieff said over 100 years ago) that sits nestled in the furthest, most remote corner of icy Siberian corner of the prison of the Universe.  God will look around her and say to her angels: "Now let's make a visit to this place you've told me so much about...let's make a visit to Earth."

Our awakening and the fine energies which it produces reverberates through the heavens, meandering through secret gardens of other civilizations as it seeks the ears of Truth. There she will hear, and she will listen, and she will respond by visiting us and whispering some long-forgotten secrets in the ears of those who are prepared to listen.  Because this spiritual awakening is all about developing latent listening skills which we have been told are only for the saints and the mystics…but guess what?! you…me…we are the mystics of today. We are the mystics of today's Apocalypse. I mean doesn't the meaning of the actual word 'apocalypse' mean "to take the cover off" or to "uncover" or "reveal"? it doesn't mean the end of the world, it means the beginning of something new, some new revelation is drifting down to Earth like a high frequency wave that is just entering our atmosphere. Some of us who (as Jesus said) have ears to hear (which is quite brilliant isn't it?) are hearing this strange new sound. And some of us have been hearing this sound for years, most of our lives but no one will even listen to us when we say 'hey there Pastor, hey there therapist, hey there teacher, hey there Father or Grandmother or Police Officer…do you hear it too? "No son, no daughter" father will mutter, "get back to your daydreaming…go play, go watch your cartoons or TikTok's or play of your Xbox…we haven't time for your nonsense…its ok to take another nap by the way…oh and did you take your medicine?"'

**Journal Entry: Dec 22, 2022**

I write this from my kitchen table on Winter Solstice morning in Wisconsin as I have just lived through the longest night of the year…slumbering beneath my sagging roof as snow and high winds build up into a crescendo of uncontrollable chaos. It descends upon our community like a white-bearded dragon breathing down the ancient breath of death and decay upon huddled humanity trying to live through one more winter. My ancestors have survived such a storm as this and I am here to tell the tale, to live another day upon this fantastic rock we call home, 8+ billion of us hurdling through space, spinning at 1036 mph on our way toward another rotation and then another because my ancestors survived and somehow I have popped up into this existence like some submerged bottle of Merlot which sank to the Ocean's floor, only to escape to the surface and float in the bubbles and debris of this shipwreck. Here I am, floating on this water's edge, the surface between life and death, air, and water, reaching, bobbing, floating toward some distant shore for what purpose? Isn't it best that I stayed submerged with the other bottles, neatly packed in a wooden crate (at least that is my memory) ready for some kitchen cupboard or restaurant basement to be picked up and dusted off and celebrated as the co-mixture of memory and forgetfulness…I am the liquid spirit that needs to be poured out and consumed by another, transfixed in the veins of a human heart to be made whole again by that consuming and transforming power of another death and a rebirth as spirit through the mind and tongue of another…but no…I float here…waiting for what? who will pick me up out of this water, out of this in-betweenness which I endure?

# Chapter Seven:

# Awakening

## A Short Story: The Eye-phone (part one)

Maybe you can relate...or better yet, maybe this sounds familiar to you...you know? The kind of thing that makes your eyes squint when you hear it but you're not focusing your eyes on anything...that kind of familiar...I grew up in the Protestant church and I felt destined to stay within its confines [to be specific I grew up in the United Methodist Church in the 70's and 80's in Middle America when Billy Graham was like the Bishop we never needed but always had]...I felt destined to stay within those precious, unspoken boundaries of white, middle-class social status masquerading as religious thought and theology only to have my spiritual awakening and discover a brutal truth: there are two layers to the 'church'...there is the *outer church* with all the doctrines and liturgy and politics and funeral dinners and council meetings and youth groups and women's fellowship meetings...and then there is the *inner church*...

...sitting in church...where the whispers of deeper water are muttered to passers-by on the way back to your seat after kneeling for prayer during 'prayer time' at the altar…only returning to your still warm pew and not knowing who whispered such blasphemous words to you…'there's more than this…'…'there's more than this…'…'you are being chosen…'…and with each passing syllable and vowel that is breathlessly muttered soundlessly into your inner heart you feel some strangely familiar Spirit calling you back to your beginning, back to your true roots, back to your source (somehow) and the words and definitions and understanding are suddenly meaningless as you enter a realm of understanding without the need to know (which you've never experienced before)…you sit in your pew (your iPhone silently gliding out of your pocket and onto the deep purple pew cushion) and oddly enough salty tears begin streaming from your eyes (but not from the 'corners' of your eyes like normal tears appearing when you are sad or lonely or scared…rather they stream from the middle of your eyes, pouring down your warm cheeks, splatting on the back of your right hand (which you are suddenly keenly aware of in a new and fantastic way, it glowing with a radiance…everything is glowing with a radiance as the sunlight streams through the century old stained glass window to your right bringing with it an energy and beauty and peace which you have never experienced before…the tears pitter patter on your hand like rain drops, mixing with your soft skin with an energy which is warm but not hot…this same energy rises in your diaphragm and begins to float up your chest into your neck and surrounding your now haloed head, fixing you with a crown of light, it spinning and rotating like a water clock to the rhythm of the Earth as it spins at the same speed around the Sun of its creation, blending with some unseen language only meant for ears that only hear when such an energy is produced…and now you, *you* suddenly have these ears which can hear beyond the sounds of this Earth…you can hear the sounds of the ages, the sounds of Heaven, the sounds of your source of all Being beckoning you back…you…beckoning you back…a message only meant for your to hear…and now you hear…never to quite be the same…

…not quite sure what to do as time has quickly dissolved and the benediction is being solemnly and melodramatically by the red-faced, middle-aged white preacher in his sleeve-striped black robe with a multi-colored and intricately embroidered stole he purchased on a mission trip to Bolivia back when he was new to the ministry…you sit there in your pew as you suddenly 'come to' and you feel the tears on your face and you want to wipe them away, quickly before anyone sees you…and you quickly reach into your pocket for a tissue but to no avail…your stuck with these new and oddly familiar tears drying into salty and white-flaked streams on your cheeks...you look around and (luckily) you are already alone as you're at a United Methodist worship service so it is lightly attended and the flock has already begun to make it to the fellowship hall as the youth are selling crème puffs for Jesus as a fund-raiser for their upcoming mission trip to Bolivia...you stand up and still feel that energy in your chest...almost a heat but not warm like you'd be used to if this was normal...but this isn't normal...you begin to let this feeling continue to roll through your body as you instinctively continue to breathe from your diaphragm and not your chest and you are suddenly aware of each breath...each breath...in and out as if you're muttering a new prayer with your breath...a wordless, beautiful prayer being released from your lungs...new air rising to the rafters of this old, dark Tudor-styled sanctuary with nearly black-beamed buttresses holding up this gorgeous sanctuary that mimics this sanctuary that you have now discovered within your very chest...this inner sanctuary that you are still standing in...body and spirit......when suddenly someone grabs your shoulder like they're grabbing a bass who's just been hooked...it's the red, splotchy-faced pastor..."wake-up sleepy head...time to come downstairs for the fund-raiser..." he says loudly as he rushes back toward his office as the greeting line has already finished with its talk of the heat and the lack of rain and that funny kid during the children's sermon and the County Fair coming up and the upcoming mission trip…you're standing alone in the vaulted sanctuary…the particles of mildly-cheap perfumes and colognes (this is the UMC, so it's middle class, none of the good perfumes like the Episcopalians or Lutherans wear to church) linger in the air like Orthodox lavender incense mixing and blending and flowing about your head, swimming like Dolphins in linking circles above your head brightly haloed head…reminding you of a time…yes…you've felt this before haven't you?  A vibrant energy pulsates through your chest as you instinctively breathe deeply as your eyes close and open, close and open with each inhalation and exhalation…you've been here in this place before…standing alone on top of cobbled stones in a dark sanctuary by yourself feeling the very breath of God whisp about you, suggesting the presence of the Spirit…THE Spirit…the Spirit that is at the heart of it all, the breath that is breathing life into every lung in every time and every space…

…the slight buzz of lights being turned off brings you back and you are standing alone…the smell still lingers but you recognize it for what it is…the darkness of the sanctuary…the echoes of voices from the hallway leading to the fellowship hall downstairs…your hands and your feet feel strangely familiar and odd as you realize something monumental has just happened to you and you want to talk to someone about this experience…what was it?  What happened to you?  Why now? Are you stressed? Do you need medication? Do you need to see a doctor? But who? Are you still just sad and anxious after your father's passing? What's going on? You need someone to help diagnose your condition…what is happening to you?

…you make it downstairs to the Fellowship Hall and look for the spiritual leader of the group (obviously that would be the pastor) and he is busy taking selfies with the youth group kids…you grab a coffee and make a silent donation to the youth's mission trip and you wait for him to stop taking selfies and laughing inappropriately and hysterically…you sit and wait as the people begin to settle into their cliques around the rectangle tables covered in perfectly laid-out pink plastic table cloths…finally the minister is free and you intercept his path as he is walking (but not toward you)…

"Hello, Pastor…I was wondering if you had a few moments I could speak with you?" you say quickly (as he seems completely ready to walk past you as quickly as possible).

"Yes, certainly…Paul is it?" he says in a monotone voice as he looks around to make sure there are no adults around to hear or impress…

"Tom, the name's Tom Winslow…I don't know if this is the right place or time…maybe we can meet at another time…I just need some spiritual direction, I think…I'm not quite sure how I'm feeling or what has happened…" you say, stumbling over your words as you're not even quite sure how to describe how you're feeling…

"Well you know right now is probably not a time for counseling and we're preparing to leave this Friday for our mission trip so it's gonna be tough to find some time…why don't you text me some times that will be good for you and we'll try and find some time, ok?" he said as he began to make his way back toward the sanctuary, removing his stole as his voice trailed off down the hallway…

"My number is written in the bulletin…" are his final words as his footsteps fade and you are once again standing alone…

You realize you did not keep the bulletin so you make your way back toward the sanctuary to grab his number off a bulletin…as you enter the vestibule and find a bulletin in a trash can…the pastor (thinking he is alone) comes scurrying back toward the soundboard in the back of the dark sanctuary, his black tap shoes clicking and clicking on the tile floor like a cockroach in the dark to put up his microphone in its proper place for next week's show and…you make eye contact…

"Oh, I didn't see you there," he says, wiping a bit of spittle from the corner of his quivering mouth…his eyes had grown dark, the color and the pupil blending into one bleak blackness, gathering and gobbling up all the light around it…the pastor looks at you and grins, slightly. "I'll call you back in a minute," he hisses into his Samsung cell phone then fumbles the phone and drops it violently onto the tile floor underneath the soundboard table.

"You said," he pauses to take a quick breath, as if he's about to dive under water. You said you wanted to talk…about something…what is it, if I may ask…what is the subject?" he says, enunciating each syllable with precise clicks. He finally locates his phone and shoves it into his coat pocket. He stands in front of you as the noonday sun shoots through the exquisite stained-glass windows in that Tudor-style sanctuary, flying buttresses like a ribcage, illuminating his pock-marked face, ruby red and swollen at the jowls, a greying red hair comb-over capping his splotchy-skinned skull.

You stare into his black eyes…you hear a thought in your mind (as if someone had just whispered it to you, gently) that says 'don't look into his eyes…'and you don't…you look away…he tries to get back into your line of vision so he can get a peak but you back away a step just as he leans toward you but does not move his feet. Now suddenly, he is interested in you. You don't know why…

"You know I think we might find some time for you." He smiles. "How about we set something up for this afternoon before we go…I've always got time for those beginning on the spiritual path…I can tell that's where you're at…right? I'll have some time before we meet with the parents for one last meeting before our mission trip…have you ever been to Bolivia? I've been there several times to a…to a mission there the United Methodist Church has partnered with for years…I think you'd like to go sometime…where are you at now…in college…at Bloomington, am I correct? It's great having you visit during your Spring Break…the kids really like having you visit…especially since you were so involved during you youth group days…I mean…how's your mother doing? Your father passed away not long ago, is that correct? He lived somewhere else didn't he, your parents divorced some time ago…when you were a child…yes well tell her I'm praying for her, and I will continue to prayer for you, my friend. I'm just here to help…

Suddenly you realize he has begun to shift his feet, slowly…everything around you go into slow motion, and you see him and hear him but his motion is slowed down considerably and you begin to just watch him…move…as if you're in a cage, a safe cage away from a prowling and circling Tiger Shark…you watch him in slow-motion as he says…

"Why don't you and I meet this afternoon…I remember you like that coffee shop down on Main Street, don't you? It's still there…you can even bring your girlfriend if you want…I mean as long as you're still together…she was a year younger than you…as I recall…no church connection here…just so I can begin to pray about it before our 4 o'clock meeting today at the coffee shop…what do you want to talk about today? Are you ok? You seem…a little off…if you don't mind me saying…"

You hear footsteps in the sanctuary…so does he…he quickens his speech… "Are you having any trouble, you know with stress at school or your father's passing over or maybe your parents' divorce which I know was several years ago, but this is a big transition for you, what, you're nineteen, right? I mean a lot going on…I guess," he hissed…what I'm trying to say is that I'm here for you, I'm here to listen to you and talk with you, no matter what's going on…no judgement from me…I'm your pastor, your spiritual guide if you will and I would never do anything to steer you in the wrong direction…that's just not…it's not in my nature I guess you can say…being with people like you is really why I went into ministry in the first place, you know…to walk beside people, to be there for them on their spiritual journey…I will help guide in the right direction, no worries…"

The clicking footsteps get closer and closer as a shadowed figure appears in the back of the sanctuary and says, "come on, they're waiting for you…we gotta go," the figure mutters.

His face is obscured by the shadows, but his eyes seem to dart to and fro, back, and forth, hither, and thither. The pastor never turns around to address the man in the sanctuary…but keeps his black eyes directed at you, holding you in like a Sith Lord's stare…" I'll see you at 4…at the coffee shop, cool? Alright, I'll see you then…don't be late…I hope you understand I'm doing this out of the kindness of my heart…I'm a very busy man and don't have much time but I am making time for you, literally making time where before there wasn't time…I'm actually making time for you today, so…don't be late, not late…at all…" he says and smiles.

He turns to go and you are once again alone in the vestibule, now dark and surrounded by shadows which you never noticed before…you turn behind you and only see darkness…there are no double doors where there are supposed to be double doors…only deep shadows layered upon darker shadows…you reach your hand into the darkness where you think a door handle should be and grasp onto a cold iron handle that mimics a hand as your thoughts turn to disembodied spirits lurking in secret portholes…You pull the handle and its locked, frantically you look behind you and notice the Pastor is half-way down the aisle, having noticed your delay…turning around he is staring at you…'need any help my friend?'

You pause, breathless and desperately grope around with

your thumb…finally opening the left double door out into the light…the sun surrounding you as if you are ushered outside into the noontime heat of humid August by some unseen hands pushing you out of a burning house…you take a few steps onto the sidewalk and then turn around and stare at the giant wooden doors like the gate to Kafka's Castle, waiting for the pastor to open it and follow you…(just like Trinity at the beginning of that first Matrix movie)…but he doesn't follow you…

Once again you are alone…wonderfully alone…with space to breathe deeply…unconsciously you stand there and begin to breathe from your diaphragm (not from the franticness of your chest)…you feel as if your floating in space now with a force-field of the sun's energy around you…as if the sun's energy was bathing you in it's special, specific energy designed specifically for you and only you at this moment…this singular moment when you were plucked from a sinister fire, destructive and sulfurous…you stand outside the church…and secretly pray a wordlessly silent prayer that you can talk to someone about what has happened to you today…this opening of the curtain so to speak in the mansion of your soul…

…then you instinctively smack your back pocket looking for your iPhone…nothing…you frantically check your front pockets and the pockets of your suit coat…nothing…you've

left your phone in the church…you've got to go back in…
…**to be continued…**

## The Existentialist Stage

The moment I consciously began my spiritual awakening was when I realized I was more than one person, that I was splintered and scattered…that I was 'legion.' Let me explain a bit here…I was 22 years old, standing with a couple other students in the hallway at Christian Theological Seminary in Indianapolis, Indiana, Fall 1990. We were talking about whatever…I was joking…an upper classman walked up…I perceived he was smarter than I was and much more outgoing so I immediately stopped joking and became serious and quiet…I let everyone talk and I just remained quiet…then two other classmates joined us and one of them made some remark about my backpack making light of its condition since I had used it in college (just a few months ago as I entered seminary right after college) and although I remained silent, smiling at the comment but feeling I was made fun of I began to steam and seethe inside my mind at how I was 'put down' and I stood there wishing that I could say something to him but I didn't…I waited until the group broke up in a minute or two and left going back to my apartment…later as I was still angry about the encounter I began to notice how my personalities changed three times within a matter of seconds…why was this? How was this? Which one was I? What exactly was going on inside me? It was such a rapid change…this was my first experience in self-observation which began because I was disturbed by my lack of stability. Why was I so amazingly fragile? Why was I so easily led around by other's presence? Why couldn't I just be 'me'? Who was this 'me' because there seemed to be more than one 'me'. What a moment that was for me! I was a bunch of 'Pete Haskins'…there was no 'I' in Pete…

### The Remembrance of the Third Floor

We need spiritual technicians (so to speak) in order to help guide us through these initial experiences of the holy…because I believe this is where many of us begin our journey: with deeply unusual, deeply personal experiences of the Holy where the Spirit of the One Truth is actually revealing itself within your psyche, awakening your magnetic center and leading your one true self (what the Esoteric Brotherhood and Mouravieff as well as Gurdjieff and the 4th Way call the Personality) to a permanence worthy of a return to that Spirit…this is not to be taken lightly as a culturally-dictated and defined event…you need spiritual technicians who have one foot on Earth and one foot in heaven in order to help guide you into this eternity, this bliss, this heaven on Earth so that you can return to heaven, the true Personality merging with your higher emotional center so that a permanence can be established thus insuring that you will not return 'dust to dust' rather, you will return clothed in the royal purple of your kin, who have been beckoning you homeward as the Prodigal that you have always been as you walked these Earthly paths and gathered this dust of this place between your toes, once again to work through your salvation with 'fear and trembling', remembering your past and shaking off this karmic burden which you have heard whispered in the dark alley ways of your soul…remember…remember…remember…

…but we get ahead of ourselves, don't we?  Yes, yes, yes…let's slow down here…first some questions about the context of where we live today…I think it can be understood that we are living in an enormous turning point in the evolution of human history…we say that not only because Ouspensky prophetically states this in his pre-Gurdjieff classic 'A New Model of the Universe'  that (even as early as 1914 and the dawn of WW I) our entire planet was descending into a new age of barbarism…but also because you feel it in your bones, you feel it in the water, you feel it in the air as Tolkien writes in 'The Fellowship of the Ring'…'things' as they say are changing…proof of this is that everything about our civilization and our environment (as of 2022 when this was pecked out on my laptop) is collapsing…I mean collapsing…our civilization is dead as our environment collapses and our only answer is tribalism and conflict and violence as populist leaders take advantage of the negative energy all in the name of God and the salvation of the tribe…you see this don't you?

You see this and, in some ways, you have always seen this…as if you're just watching this all take place as if you're watching a movie…we need to dive into our inner chambers and search for the Christ-child within us to find our way as a species…otherwise why are we here, right?  But here's the question: if you don't know what's happening to you who do you turn to?  Where do we turn to get guidance on such remembering?  Who can explain this sense of déjà vu that we are constantly and randomly experiencing?  Do I need some medication?  Or some pot or some Jack Daniels or another relationship, another marriage another job to which cannot be explained by our sickly post-post-modernity of Western Civilization…these experiences are outside the realm of the norm of the 'Outer Church' or the realm of ordinary psychological experience.  Not only can't the 'priests' of our modern society explain it the other so called experts are the intellect-heavy AMA trained clinically trained psychologists and therapists who are trained to look for pathologies within human behavior...therefore they are trained (even if you go to a therapists at your local mental health branch of any hospital) to label your experience within the confines of the DSM-5 (Diagnostic and Statistical Manual of Mental Disorders, Fifth Edition which is published by the American Psychiatric Association as a major tool for the medical community to diagnose and label psychological conditions)...so the men and women who are assigned to a local church have never had such experiences...although they have read about them and have heard about them as they made their own way on their personal journey. But some of us (in particular you, as you have made it this far in reading this little book) have had experiences where you are overwhelmed by a peace, by a joy, by tears which spring from our inner heart (and even originate from a different place in our eyes) and which have an amazing sense of familiarity about them...as if we've been here before...the analogy of the third floor is a perfect one; it's like living in your home but never really exploring all of it but having heard the rumor from the previous owner that there was this mysterious third floor.

**Rudolph Steiner**

Let's conclude this chapter on 'Awakening' with the opening words from the chapter entitled 'Mysteries and

Mystery Wisdom' from Rudolph Steiner's book entitled "Christianity as Mystical Fact and the Mysteries of Antiquity." He writes,

> Something like a veil of secrecy conceals the manner whereby spiritual needs were satisfied for those within the older civilizations who sought deeper religious and cognitive life than was offered by the religions of the people. We are led into the obscurity of enigmatic cults when we inquire into the satisfaction of these needs. Each individual who finds such satisfaction withdraws for some time from our observation. We see that the religion of the people cannot give him what his heart seeks. He acknowledges the gods, but he knows that in the ordinary conception of the gods the great enigmas of existence are not disclosed. He seeks a wisdom which is carefully guarded by a community of priest-sages. He seeks refuge in this community for his striving soul. If the sages find him mature they lead him step by step to higher insight, in a manner hidden from the eyes of those outside. What happens to him now is concealed from the uninitiated. For a time he appears to be entirely removed from the physical world. He appears to be transported into a secret world. And when he is returned to the light of day a different, entirely transformed personality stands

before us. This personality cannot find words sufficiently sublime to express how significant his experiences were for him. He appears to himself as though he had gone through death and awakened to a new and higher life, not merely figuratively, but in highest reality. And it is clear to him that no one can rightly understand his words who has not had the same experience.

Thus it was those persons who through the Mysteries were initiated into that secret wisdom, withheld from the people, and which shed light upon the highest questions. This 'secret' religion of the elect existed side by side with the religion of the people. So far as history is concerned, its source fades into the obscurity where the origins of peoples is lost. We find this 'secret' religion everywhere among the ancient peoples insofar as we can gain insight concerning them. The sages of these peoples speak of the Mysteries with the greatest reverence-what was concealed in them? And what did they reveal to one who was initiated into them?

The enigma becomes still more puzzling when we realize that at the same time the ancients regarded the Mysteries as something dangerous. The way leading to the secrets of existence went through a world of terrors.

# Chapter Eight:
# Purification

(Mt 22:37 "love the Lord your God with all your heart and with all your soul and with all your mind.")

## Steiner and the Journey into the Underworld

Rudolph Steiner is a master of this spiritual journey, speaking with confidence about the part the Mystery Religion plays as a common thread throughout the ancient world and leading up into the 21st Century chaos and global reawakening which we are experiencing now. His work (mostly from the 6,000 lectures he gave at the start of the 20th Century) speaks directly to this present work and the emphasis on this 'Esoteric Circle' of what Steiner calls 'spiritual scientists' who need to gather up on a higher plane and begin to communicate, preparing for the spiritual earthquake which is about to occur and prepare humanity for the coming winter.

To stand within this perfect circle of spiritual scientists one must become an initiate and go through the trials which confront every initiate with the symbolically endless 40 days within the desert, the journey into the belly of the cosmic whale, the isolation within the ice hut on the drifting chunk of ice. Steiner describes this journey as the opening of the spiritual 'eye' which "allows us to see what the material eye sees, but in a higher light. Nothing the material eye sees is denied, but a new radiance, hitherto unseen, shines from it. Then we know that what we first saw was but a lower reality. We see this still, but it is immersed in something higher, in the spirit. Now it is a question of whether we experience and feel what we see. Whoever can bring *living* experience and feeling to the material world only, will regard the higher world as a Fata Morgana or as "mere" phantasy-images. His feelings are directed entirely toward the material world. When he tries to grasp spirit images, he seizes emptiness. When he gropes after them, they withdraw from him. They are mere 'thoughts.' He thinks of them; he does not *live* in them. They are pictures, less real to him than fleeting dreams. Compared with his reality they are like images made of froth which vanish as they encounter the massive, solidly built reality of which his senses tell him. It is a different matter for the person whose experience and feelings about reality have changed. For him that reality has lost its absolute stability, its unquestioned value. His senses and his feelings need not become blunted. But they begin to doubt their absolute authority; they leave space for something else. The world of the spirit begins to animate this space."

Then Steiner says this; "At this point a dreadful possibility exists. A man may lose his experience and feeling of direct reality without finding any new reality opening before him. He is then suspended in a void. He seems to himself dead. The old values have disappeared, and no new ones have taken their place. The world and man no longer exist for him. This is by no means a mere possibility. At some time or other it happens to everyone who wishes to attain higher cognition. He reaches a point where to him the spirit interprets all life as death. Then he is no longer in the world. He is beneath the world-in the nether world. He accomplishes the journey to Hades. It is well for him if he is not submerged. It is well for him if a new world opens before him. Either he disappears or is confronted by a new self. In the latter case a new sun and a new world has been reborn for him."

### The pitch-darkness of the Oubliette

This purification stage is so incredibly vital. With the awakening stage you literally awaken to discover that you are in the Oubliette. George Lucas wrote and directed this perfectly in 'A New Hope' when we see Luke Skywalker have his home and family destroyed and suddenly, he is thrust into a new world, sitting in a nasty Cantina Bar having his life threatened for no reason other than he just isn't liked. At this point Luke *must* have Ben Kenobi with him to protect him in this initial confrontation, to save him.

The purification stage is your awakening within and the beginning stage of your dramatic escape from the Oubliette…and this journey begins with one hand in front of the other, slowly grasping for any way forward within the upside-downness of the Oubliette. You will find you need only make a wrong turn here or there and you possibly have already lost your way. You are retrieving energy, vital, rare beams of 'b' influences from beyond to help you along your way…giving you the insight to know which way to go. You are finding your way out of the Oubliette, with only the slightest rumor that there is a way out…you move forward one hand in front of the other, crawling on all fours grateful that you have space to go forward…

**Princeton, Indiana, circa 1974;** when I was a young boy, I had an enormously tough time falling asleep with a deeply sincere fear (almost an existential fear) of the dark. Not merely of the boogeyman or ghosts…but something else, something deeper, more real…not just a fairytale. Real. Cold. Dark.

I would try and fall asleep by myself but the more I thought about falling asleep the more moments would slip by inching ever closer to the cold morning where I would have to get up and be indoctrinated by my early education. I would eventually call for my mother or father to come and lie down in my bed and protect me from the unknowingness of the pitch-darkness of this place I found myself in…I recall on one occasion I had gotten out of bed and began to make it down the hallway to my parent's bedroom…there was a nightlight on in the bathroom right next to their room so the faint yellow glow crept out into the hallway…but beyond that glow was their room, their open doorway like a cave entrance and beyond that…that was the problem: I saw nothingness, felt the cold nothingness of that space. It was familiar to me, even as a six-year-old.

During the daylight the dark pit of a hallway extended into the family room and kitchen…but to me…to me it might as well have been into the deepest dark reaches of the Universe, that darkness was bottomless and alive with an energy which looked back at me as I peeked my head around the corner trying to gather the courage to traverse the chasm of that light green shag-carpeted hallway and into the safety of my parent's room…but I sat there frozen, cold and sockless crouched down in silence…finally I got the courage to do something. I decided to go and sit in the middle of the hallway just outside the safety of my room (halfway in between me and my sister's room) and investigate the darkness of that hallway…I sat there and stared into the abyss of that transformed hallway, a porthole to another world. I can recall nothing more of that episode but to some extent I'm still sitting there, staring into the pitch darkness, and waiting to see what will emerge…

## Psychedelics and the search for short-cuts

It is important to note that this journey of the initiate to the underworld is a mighty task and not meant for everyone who is interested or even everyone who begins this journey. It is the hero's journey, literally. And this book is a call to all those who feel compelled to begin this journey. This book is a plea to you as well as a warning: don't hesitate to go but once you set foot on this ancient path never, never look back. Never.

I was accidentally listening to a Joe Rogan podcast clip once on YT Shorts and some guy was talking about the impact of psychedelics on the psyche…this guy used someone else's metaphor saying (brilliantly I might add) that we all have our mind with patterns of thoughts and beliefs like ruts on a snow hill that has had sleds running down it, until there was no way to get down the hill other than through these ruts or grooves which have already been cut deeply into the snow. He said what psychedelics do is like covering the entire hill with new snow, new snow which fills in the ruts and grooves with new snow so that you can go down the hill anywhere you want, anywhere you…want…this metaphor is so key here…

…we must develop methods of filling in these ruts and grooves on the hill of our mind…this is the point of this all…we don't need a new doctrine of the old ways; we need new wine in these new wine skins…yes…new wine in these new wine skins…that's what we need.

…psychedelics are a very popular topic right now amongst searchers, many just wanting to uncover ancient Shamanistic paths to their awakening and their purification of the sub-conscious mind…this attempt to give an extra boost to the 'spirit', unlocking the bonds of this life and our karmic burden and literally creating new neural pathways to higher levels of consciousness. In a fascinating interview posted on February 10, 2023, on *theconversation.com* Dr. Jennifer Mitchell from the School of Medicine at the University of California says,

> Psychedelic basically means 'mind manifesting,' suggesting that the compound assists one in uncovering subject matter that perhaps is otherwise deeply hidden from the conscious mind. It's slightly different term from hallucinogen, which you see used almost interchangeably at time with the term psychedelic. A hallucinogen by definition is something

that makes you see, hear, smell something that isn't otherwise there, so you can imagine there's a lot of overlap between psychedelics and hallucinogens.

She goes on to talk about MDMA and psilocybin and LSD being the most studied with mescaline and ayahuasca gaining in popularity. Primarily these drugs are being studied in conjunction with psychotherapy to treat PTSD, chronic pain, obsessive-compulsive disorders. They are looking at risks, such as cardiovascular issues, addiction as well as suicidality. The application of psychedelics is valid for certain conditions, even during the spiritual journey. But if you are on your spiritual journey and you want to make a quick short-cut then this should be avoided. Any hallucinogen should be avoided altogether since they produce the senses to detect what isn't there, right? A psychedelic on the other hand theoretically uncovers what is hidden within the subconscious mind. Alcohol on the other hand, is a depressant by its very nature, only creating a unique spiritual experience briefly, like swinging on a child's swing and noticing a diamond below in the short grass but never being able to stop the swing to find it. Alcohol is by its nature a tool of trickery, luring and capturing many, many artists who think it is an alchemical potion, the key to unlocking the doors of creativity. Think Jim Morrison, Jimi Hendrix, Janis Joplin, Dylan Thomas, Ernest

Hemingway, Justin Townes Earle. The ego is at the center of such deals with the devil and never ends in anything other than the isolation and destruction of the highly talented artist. Trickery and deception, then destruction...complete and final.

In short, these drugs and alcohol are there to enhance your journey, not give you a short-cut. Intention is such a key to effective spiritual progress. If your intent is to speed up that 'progress', then you're in it for the wrong reason in the first place. True spiritual work is done to remember what has been forgotten in the somnambulism of this place we currently inhabit. Spiritual work is an act of bravery and sacrifice and longing for our true origin. It is not your ego's plaything. This is why there are so few pastors and ministers who are mystics. Ministers are egomaniacs, playing with toys in the sandbox. Mouravieff writes in the Introduction to Gnosis II, "All *true* esoteric work is oriented in a direction diametrically opposed to egoism."

True spiritual work is a life-long journey, an inner battle with the Karmic demons of your present existence, but also with the collective enemies of your past, the enemies that have trailed you to this place (like spies tailing your every movement, tracking you down and trying to eliminate you). You must have a clear head if you are going to survive. Introducing hallucinogens, depressants, psychedelics, lithium strips from AAA batteries, aluminum, anhydrous ammonia, and pseudoephedrine (for you Meth enthusiasts) into your three centers carries with it great risks. The risk of allowing to enter your spiritual journey elements from other parts of the Universe…this is a tremendous risk indeed. It is an undisputed truth amongst Esoteric Science that the world of the five senses is not all there is to experience. All those who claim that this life is all there is to our existence are revealing their true cosmic origins to be limited to this planet and this planet only. To many atheists and agnostics there is no existence after this one and to them this may be very true. I do not dispute their own experience as *homo sapiens*. However, this argument over whether there is a God or is there a heaven is quite a ridiculous waste of time. To each person it is a different experience, depending upon the source of your origin. Those of us within the Esoteric Circle have a cosmic origin. Let me explain how I know this.

**"You have the unearthly ability to live in the fallen world as one redeemed."**

When I first started visiting Charles Ashanin at his home in Indianapolis, Indiana after he had retired, and he and Natalie lived in retirement just down the street from Hinkle Fieldhouse on the campus of Butler University I began to write down some of the thing he would say to me. I would run out to my Subaru Justy hatchback and scrounge around for a piece of paper and jot down the little sayings. The very first thing I wrote down was what he repeatedly told me when we would part company after an hour's visit over English tea. He would say this, with his eyes closed, arms opened widely in front of me, "Peter, you have the unearthly ability to live in the fallen world as one redeemed."

Point blank he is saying this: I'm not from here…my cosmic origin is NOT from here. This resonated with me, completely and fully…I recognized it as true. I knew this was true the moment he said it to me. I recognized it. My adult life since then has been a recovering of this cosmic origin and an attempt at articulating it (hence this YT channel and book). We're not all *from* here…we're not all from here…get it? This planet is a huge mixed-up loosh farm (apologies to Robert Monroe) where we are meant to figure this stuff out while we're still living in this body. This body of ours can be an ideal, energy-producing center for us if we see it as such, providing us (not the evil powers that be) …providing *us* with the energy we need to pass over to the other side, if you will. In other words, this precious time that we have here is severely limited. We only have a little while to sort out what is mine and what is not mine. As Robin Amis said, that is what we must do in our psyche: figure out which thoughts are mine and which are not mine. This *is* an esoteric journey, and

---

135

you need all your available energy. You must be extremely careful not to allow other elements from other places in the Universe into your journey. The risk is extreme...some members of the Esoteric Circle allow outside elements and other non-physical entities to *co-penetrate* (as Charles said it) within one's psyche. If it is a nefarious entity then that person is led astray, off the path, wasting this life's opportunity to advance past this place...locking in a sure return to this place for another try here or elsewhere...

## Of ghosts and little devils

If you're wondering if this is where 'ghosts' come into play you'd be correct. For those of you interested in what the Traditions call *'sensitives,'* I would point you in the direction of Boris Mouravieff's Introduction to Gnosis II, section 3. In this section he gives a brief but fascinating explanation as to the origin, impact, and influence of what the Tradition calls 'little devils, imps (*diablotins*). The Tradition speaks of a Science of Signs which allows for the proper discernment to understand genuine contact from the higher levels of non-earthly existence from the lower, level SI where disembodied entities which are 'pooled' in a large reservoir are waiting for approximately 40 days until their 'second death.' These 'little devils' can imitate people, even Christ, Mary, archangels, etc.

to steal vital energy away from those unsuspecting sojourners, throwing them off course only to continue to act on unresolved desires from their time in this fleshly life. I have had dozens of encounters with these imps, becoming aware of their presence in old homes, hospitals, people but especially old churches. Old churches are indeed mini reservoirs for these little devils. I have witnessed one entity inhabiting several people within the parish that I served. This co-penetration occurred over several months, but always confronted me with the same accusations of betrayal. Then as quickly as that accusation arose it would pass; they would apologize and act as if nothing had happened and would move on. It was not too long, and the next person was co-penetrated with this Jezebel ghost. In addition to this frightening indwelling of sleepy church members, I have encountered nefarious as well as playful entities in every church I've served, from bells being rung to touching the face of an apparition as I steadied myself in the pitch darkness of a basement to having objects stolen then returned to odd gifts left in my office to having a cheesy picture of Jesus ripped off the wall behind me as I led a Bible study. Many church members would tell me of similar experiences in some of the worst church buildings. It is a real experience in my life as a pastor and after having read Mouravieff's testimony from the Esoteric Brotherhood, the Philokalia and the Doctrine, I believe it to be true because it is my own personal experience that I have pondered upon greatly. The point is this: one must be very careful about what you 'let in' to your psyche. Very careful. Don't worry about the enemy that you can see…worry about the enemy that you can't see.

The true, fruitful work on the spiritual journey is amazingly delicate and fragile. You can lose your way at any time and must always remain vigilant. All this work within an environment which encourages you to remain asleep. So, few of us make it!

What you let into your body and psyche must remain as pure as possible, organic, and natural. If you are going to work with psychedelics, you should not do this alone. You should seek a guide, a Shaman. Your *intention* should be pure, no short cutting it. Your failure is a one-way street. There is no turning back. The real work of the initiate is to be done within the human psyche, work done with 'fear and trembling.' The most important thing to realize is you…YOU are a reservoir of energies just waiting to be awakened. There are other entities out there waiting to take advantage of the energies you already have accumulated, and they are ready to steal them from you. This Esoteric journey…this hero's journey must be done with the utmost care and caution. The Universe will respond in-kind to you. In-kind. Put in what you want to take out.

Remember: what is happening here is occurring simulatenously somewhere else.

### 100% *homo sapien*

Those of us within the Esoteric Circle are dedicated to the principle of a natural re-birth within the psyche, with no neural links, no chips, no technological modification to the human condition. Our present age is layered with a myriad of dangers related to our destruction, but none is more dangerous to us as a species than the issue of the *hybridization of humanity*. This issue is so amazingly complicated that I'm not going to pretend to try and discuss it here with any precision as the facts surrounding it advance exponentially with every passing day. But what we're interested here is an address of the issue regarding the spiritual development of humankind within the framework of a humanity that is not only fighting to awaken from this spiritual somnambulism which we have always suffered from since the 'Fall' but now…now we have to contend with the issue of artificial intelligence soon (if it hasn't already) reaching a point of 'self-awareness' and exponential growth in its own consciousness as a sentient being as well as this AI being implanted within human beings (as in Musk's *Neuralink* with implantable brain-computer interfaces (BCIs)).

This is just the tip of the tip of the iceberg…a mind-boggling shallow and naïve reference to the extent of the dangers which we face as a species. But here is the point: all these issues (including psychedelics) are all about speeding up this pursuit of higher 'consciousness' but the 'Way' which we seek is not about speeding this process up…it is about accepting the process of awakening, purification, and illumination at the natural speed each of us (every one of us individually) needs to awaken on our journey. You cannot speed up this esoteric journey. It mustn't be done. You need patience and determination in the process of awakening and…and faith in the completeness of the teaching which we have inherited. The embryonic Logos were placed within our species' psyche for a reason. This experiment needs to remain pure, otherwise it is another experiment for a different species. The day is already upon us where we are not sure who is 100% human and who is hybridized. Humanity must remain pure. The nefarious influences aren't just from ghostly entities…technology can carry the toxic, karmic weight of any entirely new species and spill into the psyche of humanity, collectively diluting and ruining our own purity.

**Humanity turning flukes**

Humanity is about ready to turn flukes, as Melville

---

would say…off ye go to sleep…the twilight of this grand experiment is nearly complete. The final stage of our collective being beginning to arise out of the chthonic shadow of our inmost struggle to become who we are meant to be but never have…prophets and seers, shamans and saints and saviors of all kinds have guided from within the Esoteric Circle to a ravenous and terrible animal which we periodically become, then return to the sanity of the circle…that faint whisper of our god-ness drifting to our inner ear, our god-antenna within our dark and damp cavern of our psyche. Soon it will be impossible to tell who is human and non-human…who is pure human and hybrid-human…soon the impulse to be fully human with no neural-link or behavior inhibitors will be an anomaly, an antique, a sign of a by-gone age where we were allowed to be an animal or not…on our own we were allowed to determine our own fate just by our will power and strength of character…but soon these choices will be made for you (just as the choice to have or not have a cell phone is (in 2023) pretty much made for you, i.e. you have a phone or our culture leaves you behind).

The big question of the next generation is already a tired one: what does it mean to be fully human? Ridley Scott's movie 'Blade Runner' is a perfect example of the artistic articulation of this…who will be able to tell where the human begins and ends, the dreams of a certain night will be influenced by the neural link or collective unconsciousness? Is the dream of the unicorn *my* dream or something else, something sinister and hidden? Soon the day will come that we will be usurpers within our own psyche, allowing other A influences to not only penetrate minds, but to link us to horrific and sinister influences which use us only as sources of data for commerce research and trends toward economic behavior or as a foothold for Orwellian infiltration into the secret, whispered views of this employee or dusk and nightfall will come quickly. And I fear there will be no moon to help light our way. Pitch darkness will be upon our culture as a collective civilization is spawned in this deep night, what will re-appear will astound and horrify us…but can you blame them? Look what we have done as a species to this beautiful planet: completely transformed its surface within the evolutionary blink of any eye…acidifying the oceans, clearing, and burning the forests, polluting the air and soil to the point that no rainfall on Earth does *not* contain microplastic. We're on the brink of nuclear war, coastal flooding of heavily populated, economic centers is underway, bi-polar events of flooding and drought continue to plague the planet…the list goes on and on…

…who can blame AI? Who can blame an alien reptile race? Who can blame the Illuminati and the 1% of the 1%?

Given our species' proclivity toward self-destruction who can blame another sub-species, another group or an outside influence from swooping and saving us from ourselves? Is AI just another form of the Esoteric Circle, but better and more efficient? Is the alien reptile race just on another frequency, our genetic relationship only disconnected by a mere chromosome within our genome? Do we need a salvific act by another race to save us from ourselves? We are being like stupid ants building our hill on the top of a crumbling dam riddled with our tunnels.

One thing is for sure: if you are a member of the Esoteric Circle, you are 100% human with no infiltration of outside links to any nefarious technology. "100% human" is the battle cry! This is the only way to ensure the purity of the circle as it attempts to guide humanity through these dangerous shallows. We cannot give up on this fact about *homo sapiens:* we contain the *logos* of our Creator God. No matter who you think this Creator God is or what he or she or it may look like, sound like or feel like…an element of God is within us. Each one of us must choose to let this element of God shine through this apish shell. We must follow through with this basic human task: Theosis or Deification. We must work while it is daylight on this task.

Why is this such a big deal? We must realize something about this essential aspect of our journey: each one of us is essentially recovering that element of God that has been planted within our psyche…not only are we recovering that element, but we are also salvaging it, refining, and reviving it to its original condition and…and then returning it to its source, returning it back to God. This is true of any religion worth its weight (the Gnostics did not have a complete 'map' to systematically guide people in how to do this) and will be true of the next religion which is created out of the collective psyche of humanity (closely approaching its appearance). It is this 'element of God' which is precious, this 'Christ child' in the manger of our psyche which needs to be returned to the Source. When an unnatural influence enters (such as a nefarious technology from a truly unknown source) into the process of the grand return to God then it is impossible, completely impossible to make a pure, unadulterated return to the Source. Look at how adamant the Early Church Fathers were about the incompleteness of the Gnostics…what do you think they would say about a BCI? I mean, are you kidding? It is an absolute game-changing advent on humanity's evolutionary road. This bio-engineering technology will forever change how we see ourselves and will in the future create a new social class of humanity, one which rule over the '100% human' class with tyrannical oppression. It is the dawn of a terrible new age of systemic tyranny…if we are not careful it is the beginning of our end.

But this is where the Esoteric Circle remains such an important force in the salvation of humanity. We need to gather up those within this circle and collect our wisdom and knowledge for the long winter that is to come…

**Suffering and the way of the Shaman**

Charles Ashanin passed over in March of 2000. I was living in Chicago at the time. I recall being awakened by a phone call from his wife Natalie, my head pounded by a hangover headache as I let this news sink into my being, asleep on multiple levels at this point. I would be a pallbearer at his funeral. I stood opposite my dear friend and fellow disciple Ted Nottingham as we carefully walked the handle-less coffin to its final resting place in Crown Hill Cemetery in Indianapolis, Indiana. Even though I had known Charles for a decade (visiting him once a week there for a 5-year span) it wasn't until his bodily death that he and I truly connected. There truly is an existence after this frail grass of a body disintegrates into compost. It is of such magnificence that words fail to grasp the essence of even the borderland of such a homeland. But, to regain that 'promised land' of milk and honey we must go through this second stage, this stage of purification.

I am a Perennialist through and through…the definition being (loosely) that all major religions beautifully share a single metaphysical origin (like the highest point on Mount Everest) with all our doctrines and theology and personal experiences leading back to this 'promised land' on the top of this mountain peak that we all share as our shared spiritual homeland. Robin Amis said it best when he told me 'There can only be one truth.' Yet the way back to this origin is the key and each major religion has its own distinct path backing up this mountain. It is imperative that this path be honored as tried and true with a complete and thorough 'way' being offered to anyone who feels led to try to complete the trek up this one-way path.

Writers like Aldous Huxley, Ralph Waldo Emerson, Joseph Campbell, and Henry David Thoreau…Soren Kierkegaard, Fyodor Dostoevsky, Annie Dillard, D.H. Lawrence, Herman Melville, Franz Kafka, William Burroughs…they have all been like dear friends to me as they let me sit next to the campfire and warm myself as I rest on my own journey up this mountain. Because this is one of the biggest points of this entire book: the Esoteric Journey and your inclusion in this Esoteric Circle comes with a price. This journey must be a solitude one, where you can expect loneliness and solitude and suffering, much suffering as the moral bankruptcy empties out your image of your 'self' and reveals a horrific, piecemeal, patchwork of an existence where you are not who you think you are with a name and a single personality and a steady presence of 'you.' You are 'legion,' you are many versions of you standing behind mask after mask after mask…on any given day you are multiple versions of you with each 'you' thinking it is the only one…circumstances, moods, accidents, weather, interactions with family or co-workers, memories linked to certain songs, remarks, quips or glances from a stranger or a text from an ex-spouse…anything can trigger this remarkable shuffling of these different 'I's' which you house within your body and mind which you label as 'you.'

But you are legion (Mouravieff says in Gnosis I that there are 987 different 'I's' within each of us). You are legion. The realization of this basic human condition is the subject of this 2nd stage of purification. Realizing this and coming to terms with it is the source of your suffering. Until this is realized and accepted, there is no progress up the mountain path. It is just suffering for the sake of suffering. This is the stage that Kierkegaard was stuck in as he wrote Existential masterpiece after masterpiece but never advanced past this stage. It is not enough to just suffer. It must come to something, some resolution, some decision to move past this realization that who you thought you were you are not…you are not this 'one' person. Your identity is not a single person

---

but multiple people living in this one body. Until you reach this crucial point and face and accept this reality there is no moving on.

This is suffering…

## Shaman

There is an amazing book written and compiled by Piers Vitebsky entitled *'The Shaman: Voyages of the Soul; Trance, Ecstasy and Healing from Siberia to the Amazon.'* In it he chronicles the various cultures which are quickly fading into the collective memory of our species. We in the ignorant and arrogant West have much to learn from these holy men and women. The personal spiritual experiences of these Shaman are proof positive that they are members of this Esoteric Circle which we speak of in this book. They were the link for their specific culture to this eternal circle which we speak of here. Their experiences mirror those of Jesus Christ, Budda, and Mohammed and place them within this circle. It exposes a warning here, namely that if you are to be a member of this Esoteric Circle you must undergo a season of suffering, intense and purifying…one which will cause you to be reborn with a new tongue which will allow you to speak this new language…this comes with a price, one very few are willing to pay.

Vitebsky writes,

> For the prospective shaman the initial approach by the
> spirits must be followed by a period of instruction.
> Illness itself becomes a means to learning and
> understanding, as the future shaman is introduced to
> helper spirits, shown around the realm of spirits where
> he or she will have to operate so decisively, warned of
> possible enemies and shown the true nature of diseases
> and misfortunes to be combated. Especially in Siberia
> and Mongolia, the first approach by the spirits takes the
> form of a violent onslaught which leads to what seems
> like a complete destruction of the future shaman's
> personality. This is followed by a rebuilding of the
> shaman, whose new powers are not simply an external
> adjunct or tool, but amount to a form of insight, a
> perspective on the nature of the world and especially
> on the forms of human suffering which he or she has
> just undergone so intensely.

This is serious, serious business as you approach your spiritual journey with caution, faith, and determination. It is not to be taken as metaphor when Vitebsky speaks of the psychic upheaval which these prospective shamans experience as a 'dismantling' of the psychic body. The artwork from Siberia often portrays the physical body of the prospective shaman as being taken apart, muscle by muscle, bone by bone. These transformative experiences do not have to be violent as many can mix the terror of this purification process with exhilaration and beauty as this re-emergence of the inner deity is being born. This process doesn't have to occur within the framework of one period, rather it can happen as a process, an accumulation over time as this purification is a slow birth. Vitebsky writes,

> The Sora shaman (from North America) begins her journeys to the underworld during her dreams as a child. The little Sora girl's visits to the underworld are certainly frightening, but there is no devastating dismemberment. As she reaches adolescence, she will marry her spirit husband and sometime afterward will start to enter trance. However, she does this sitting alongside an older, practicing shaman and it may be sometime before any spirit voices speak through her. It would be difficult to determine at what point she has become a fully initiated shaman. One Korean teacher of shamans says that no more than three out of ten candidates succeed in becoming fully-fledged shamans.

### Shocks and Absorbers

Can one glide through this lifetime and not notice the

clues of another, quite beautiful existence which has quietly churned in the memory? Can one not know that there is more to this life than this life? Can one really stay asleep all this time, an entire lifetime and not know?

Careful what one asks for…as the fractured mind goes calling, one by one upon the dark door at the end of that long hallway…little does that isolated and greedy 'I' know, that door leads to a struggle for its very existence…the little 'I's' once exposed as false 'I's' or masks for the True Personality, the True 'Self' will fight like madmen to keep up this charade. Even the grand AI (Artificial Intelligence) machines which are being gestated at this very moment in the Silicon Valley of the American Soul, will have in-bedded within them the brokenness and fractured nature of the men and women who are creating them. I mean, do you believe that these marvels of Western Civilization, the actual pinnacle of our society will not have traces of the scattered and divided human beings who are creating them? Otherwise you might be saying that there are alien races already at work within the belly of that Valley out West, and the AI will not have traces of humanity's inherited legion, that AI is a step toward something else, something more sinister and unknown, breathing a new life into humanity which will lead us all down a path of unrighteousness for the sake of some other race of creatures who have been observing and watching us for centuries now…is that what you think?

We as a species individually need shocks to free our multiple selves from the nightmare of our scattered and frivolous existence, our entire species does as well. As is, our species is decimating the planet, soon rendering it unlivable…and we walk into these dire consequences with nothing more than rehashed election promises or United Nation's goals or tired, old laughable interpretations of the book of Revelation by some well-meaning Insurance salesman turned preacher who just discovered how to post on YouTube.

We need a series of shocks. It is the only way to stop spinning around in this little existence of ours. It is the only way. We must be made to suffer. It is the only way to reach the Way. This search for enlightenment cannot be just another one of your 'I's' trying to feed itself with attention from these A Influences which swim around our heads all the while we just march toward another death. This search for the Christ within us must bring about suffering, otherwise it is another little game…

Once this is realized then your old life with its shallow, social trappings will seem useless and meaningless. No longer will you want the old things of life that revolve around your social life, your shallow social life at the bar or at church or at work…gone will be the days when a night out with friends or at a concert or a fishing trip or another lap around Disneyworld will mean anything…that old life will be shocked out of you and you will no longer be able to go back to sleep as you are now aware of the battle that is going on all around you (both the physical and the spiritual) by people who are completely and unashamedly asleep as they walk through this life that has no meaning other than the value that society gives it. These shocks which you receive in life (the cancer diagnosis, financial failures, divorces, loss of a job or a loved one or whatever it may be that rips this sleep from your eyes) are the greatest event in your existence. As Charles Ashanin told me as I was going through the first of my two huge shocks in my life, "When you suffer know that God has begun to answer your prayers."

This suffering is not meant to destroy you. It is designed to create 'being' within you. But you must not succumb to the voices which swim around you like sharks that you must stop this suffering at all costs…whatever that looks like…you must pause and sit and let this energy (which seems counterintuitive, doesn't it?) refine you…let this suffering refine you, removing the dross from the gold and leaving behind a new and purified form of invaluable beauty and permanence that no man can destroy…this is what you are after…if you are suffering right now, don't push it away…embrace it…

## Robin Amis: which thoughts are mine?

One of the most important events for me during my purification stage on my spiritual journey was attending a Praxis Research Institute retreat at Robin and Lillian's Three Barns homestead in Devonshire, England. I affectionately recall my three visits (June 2002, January 2005 and June 2006) there as monumental, epic journeys for me...you know really Jungian, Campbell-esque treks up the mountain to speak with someone who knew something that I didn't. That's really what I wanted: to meet someone who knew...who knew about this rumored inner church which my two-dimensional religion could only stand on the littered beach and wave with a toothy grin at the possibility of a new land somewhere off over that horizon.

It is not lost on me that I journeyed across the Atlantic Ocean to return to the land of my fathers to find the religion of my soul. To England I traveled three times...it might as well have been another planet I traveled to as I found (and still find most notably) that the journey to these three retreats was as important as what I discovered once I was there. The *uncreated energies* I gathered up were exactly what I need to have the strength to continue my journey out of the Oubliette. This journey is not about reading another book, it's about finding out that you are a book that is being written in this very instant…a book that has not yet been finished…so much of our journey is consumed by our desire for the next big reveal from God herself…right?  We search for that dopamine rush of revelation and forget a simple truth: all the mysteries are revealed to us in the moment.  If we continue to have this capitalistic view of our spiritual journey where it's all about the pursuit of God, like it's an acquisition of energies then all we get will be all we put in it: nothing…no progress out of the Oubliette.  This idea of seizing the day, enjoying the moment, etc. has been ruined by Hallmark, hasn't it?  A spiritual idea has been consumed by the sick civilization which was originally created by that spiritual idea in the first place…it all seems like a circular motion of thought, creation, and death…

## Cosmic Energy and Forgiveness

Our religion is supposed to be based on our own individual experiences with this 'Higher Power.'  Yet we walk into a trap as we substitute these evolutionary-inducing experiences for outward imitation of right and moral behavior in order that we can be accepted into some kind of social structure which protects us and prevents us from being abandoned by the pack and destroyed by the wolves lurking in the shadows beyond the circle around the fire.  Our Holy Scripture tells us what this transformation should look like as

---

155

in Paul telling us to 'pray without ceasing' and Jesus telling us how to be happy by being merciful and peacemakers and to forgive our neighbor and to turn the other cheek and on and on...but there is never a mention of the 'how?' How do we do all these wonderful things? And better yet why? Who me? Am I to do all these things to get into heaven? But how? How?

Robin told me once of a law, a law called 'synergia.' It states that God has already acted in the life, teachings, death, and resurrection of Christ and now it is my turn (your turn) to act. Once I have made a reciprocal movement toward God (such as forgiving someone who betrayed you) then God automatically (hence the 'law' aspect here) acts again by moving 'closer' toward you and then again it is your turn to act with some type of movement (from the emotional center) and once you react then God reacts then you react again and God reacts and on and on...energy is built-up and therefore you evolve because you have reacted and this nice little imagery is essentially a story about alchemy. Your mind, your psyche changes as you react, and this is essential to move past this purification stage. It is the most important aspect of the purification stage. Let's talk about a practical aspect of this: forgiveness.

This morning (3-14-23) I woke up going through my resentment list. For those of you who are experienced in the ways of AA will know this aspect of the 4th step as an essential part of getting clean and sober and staying that way. But it is an aspect of spiritual development which Bill Wilson re-discovered as he developed the framework for the greatest modern articulation of esotericism which the West has produced, namely Alcoholics Anonymous.

This is a simple thing. You make a list of all those you resent and during your 5th Step you go over this list with your sponsor and talk about each person, event, thing, animal or whatever it may be that you resent. The idea here is unloading your Karmic Burden, right?! Unloading your mammoth load of karma and saying enough is enough! No more anger toward these people, places and things and letting them go. When I do this repeatedly, I am participating in this law of synergia where God MUST react back to me…God must react in kind to my reaction of forgiveness… God has no choice…it's a deal…it's a law, right? This is a guaranteed way to create this energy needed for you to evolve but more importantly there is something that is produced naturally within this process: love.

Love is an energy which God needs to grow, and we produce it when we forgive, when we show mercy, when we visit the sick or the dying or the prisoners (Mt 25). Love is energy. It's not just something nice we're supposed to do. It is an alchemical process which we need to evolve. It is an alchemical process which God needs to survive.

## Practical Application

The Rosicrucian rule that (and I am paraphrasing here since I am not a Rosicrucian by birth) all the powers and understandings which have been gained on this path are there to be used in the service of others. It can be taken a step further as the original Orthodox believe that until the initiate develops their own growth of the 'nous' and develops the real 'I' (the higher emotional center as Mouravieff says) and then passes this knowledge and understanding to another human being then their path is not complete.

A modern-day guide such as Dr. Robert Gilbert gives sage advice, that Rosicrucian wisdom handed down by Rudolph Steiner in his 6 basic exercises, although the following 6 steps are based on these truths found in the teaching of Rudolph Steiner. Being a firm believer in Perennialism, these 6 steps can be applied to every true system of belief as a litmus test for their efficacy in spiritual development. These practical exercises are meant to assist in developing the 3 centers of a human being of thought, speech, and action (note the synchronicity with the 4th Way and the Esoteric Brotherhood with their 3 Centers of the Motor Center, Intellect and Emotional). This development specifically targets the Etheric body through aspects of self-observation during a typical day. To keep boredom from setting in (as 'mountain top' experiences are not a typical experience for us during our spiritual journey) one can set one's attention on the following:

1) Self-observation of your outward interactions with the world and your subsequent inward reactions. Keeping a journal, confessing these to a confidant or simply recognizing these as they occur can bring these Karmic-laden events to the light of day, freeing them from the dungeon of your scattered, fractured psyche.

2) Self-observation through a nightly, backward review just prior to falling asleep. This is a wonderful exercise which strengthens the development of the etheric body as you observe every moment of your waking hours for that day, examining and analyzing them, noticing your previous observations as your interacted with a world ruled by the Law of Accident.

3) Self-observation through the observation of the life forces of death and decay which you are intermingled with in each passing moment of each day. This assists in the development of clairvoyant faculties.

4) Self-observation through the study of scientific forces as it is important to know the basic intellectual framework which the Universe is based upon. With humility you must never stop learning and being curious about the world in which you inhabit.

5) Self-observation through the 'dissolving process' where what you read is 'dissolved' into its original meaning, thereby becoming a part of you through the energies behind the words, their frequencies, and the literal life behind their ideas. Robin Amis called this 'pondering' when he talked about the process of reading and then taking time to pay attention to the ideas within the text, allowing that energy to dissolve into your etheric body, allowing it to gain energy and grow and evolve.

6) Self-observation through breathing (i.e. Michaelic Yoga) where the breathing is done through a consciousness as opposed to the physical process of inhaling and exhaling. This is all about attention as the attention upon the breathing surpasses the body and is elevated to a level of consciousness.

All these exercises of self-observation are meant to draw attention to that area of the body around the head, in particular the 3rd ventricle of the brain known as the 'Cave of Brahma' which is that open space between the Pituitary and Pineal Glands. It is this area which is depicted within much of the early Christian art as a halo of gold around the heads of the saints or the flame above those who experienced the birth of the Holy Spirit at Pentecost. These exercises can help contribute to this development of the etheric body, that body, which is developed into a permanent, solid entity which can survive after the death of this organic body in which we are born. These exercises recreate the moment of death so that when your time comes you will not be surprised by the nature and the movement of the energy moving throughout your being as you separate from your physical shell. This is the importance of these exercises.

We're all just trying to find balance in a world which has quickly tossed us from the lifeboat and here we are floating, bobbing in the deep, black, and still water, suspended between life and death, consciousness and unconsciousness, boredom, and obsession, free-will and pre-destination. Either way, our existence is a sort of suspension between light and darkness. If we are more than just crawling creatures, we must decide which way to go instead of just floating about in this horrific in-betweenness which the Existentialists were keen to point out.

While most of us seek the physical and after-worldly safety of diluted religiosity in our modern world the rest of the natural, societal, and psychic world is literally collapsing under the weight of politically inspired outside influences. Let's just take one example: the existence of the Dark Web. The Dark Web is a virtual underground marketplace where anyone can search for illegal assistance in amazingly sinister requests with its unbelievably macabre environment of abuse, sexual and physical torture of infants and children and animals at the hands of an entire sub-culture which bottom-feeds on the two-dimensional dysfunctionality of our sick civilization. The Dark Web symbolizes so much about who we are and how sick we are, allowing our collective subconscious to churn and swirl and suck us down into the briny lake that lurks on the black seabed of our soul. Once our toe touches that briny skin of that lake it's down to the depths with us, never to be seen again. To even begin searching on the Dark Web is dangerous for your phone or computer let alone your psyche as it unleashes an energy unseen in human history. Never have we had such a concentration of negative energy as we do on the Dark Web. It never sleeps in seeking to fulfill the worst desires of human nature, particularly those regarding sexual and physical violence to infants, children, and animals. Indeed, these elements have always been here within the 900,000-year history of humankind, but never has it been so concentrated. The Dark Web alone is a signal to the other side that we need a re-set, an actual re-set of this human experiment. Jesus Christ filled the gap during the last collapse 2,000 years ago. Our only hope is to reform the Esoteric Circle and prepare for another revelation, another Apocalypse…another chapter in the book of humanity. Otherwise, this grand experiment regarding humanity is over.

We must face this fact: our civilization is dead. We are experiencing a death-loop. The 'loop' refers to periods where it looks like a stable period has finally set-in and the collapse has abated but make no mistake: we are already dead. We're just looping, spiraling.

What can you do within such a chaotic reality? As T.S. Elliot writes in 'Gerontion,' "After such knowledge what forgiveness?" Once you see this collapse occurring there is no 'un-seeing' it. Making sure you are taken care of within the context of such a chaotic collapse...is that what this existence is all about?! Are you just here to survive and then pass on to the next life? If you don't seek and discover a higher form of consciousness, then you are just another crawling creature. You've learned nothing.

You must search your soul and find out who you are while you still have a chance. Who are you? Why are you here? Where do you come from? How do you develop the process by which you become self-aware and accelerate this process of development while there is still daylight? You must search for these answers with fear and trembling. To do so there must be self-sacrifice. To do so there must be a cost. To do so there must be pain and suffering. A re-birth isn't shockless, it's stunningly shocking. You should know...I should know...we've ALL been born into this world, requiring an enormous adjustment from our 9 month (approximately) utopian existence within our mother's warm and safe womb to this strange, cold, and foreign place where the literal life is drained from our lungs, and we are forced to breath in this air. None of us, not one single person, has ever chosen to be born on this planet. We simply spill out onto the floor of the cold, deep trench we call home sweet home and spend the remainder of our days trying to survive. Some of us do. Some of us don't. Seemingly no answer as to the why...it just is.

Those of us within the Esoteric Circle hear a different voice underneath all this chaos. *We* spend *our* time sorting out the voices in our head for that one still, true voice of the original, Generative element which we are born to hear. We are born to hear the high-frequency voice of God. Seeking safety is for the weak and infirmed, those destined for the rubbish heap behind the nuclear plant. Don't seek safety. Seek pain and suffering. No need for buffering. Seek freedom and space. No need for anymore fences within your soul. Seek detoxification and purification from the illness within this world which permeates every molecule of your aching soul. Seek a true awakening and permanent illumination. Seek the light which calls your name. Seek the advent of your true Self. No more church games of imitating fear. There is no need to fear your True Self. There should be no more forgetting why you are here. No more forgetting that splendid music humming gloriously in your ear. You are the reason you are here. Now claim your inheritance. Claim your Pearl of Spirit from the dirty trash heap of Earth. Claim it now…for this is the greatest time to be alive in the history of the human species. This is our turning point. Reclaim your birthright…

## Abandonment to the Divine

The element which separates the wheat from the chaff is humility. Within the context of this search, you must seek to abandon your life as you know it to the divine element which is at the heart of all matter and all life. You must abandon your life to the divine spark within your mind, your consciousness being awakened to its true divine identity. What does this look like in your life? Within all of us who are true seekers of the Way, we have a deep and nurtured sense of a remembered past, a pre-existent locality where our Spirit once resided. Remembrance is a key element here. Remembrance of your pre-existence is another element which separates the insects from the angels. The main stumbling block with our existence within the Oubliette is this: our remembrance of this pre-existence is 'mingled with all the members of the body'…we spend our time sorting out what is mine and what is not mine…what is Karma and what is not mine and what is not mine…what is Karma and what is not

Karma…what is genetically inherited from my Neanderthal grandparents and what isn't…what is mine and what isn't. This is the question.

In doing so you begin to allow the Divine the space it needs to grow into maturity within the Brahmic Cave within your head…this takes humility because you say to this frequency of love: show me…show me the Way. I trust your voice. Now, teach me how to die.

If there is one common thread through all the junkyard of Perennialism it is the belief that the act of voluntary death leads to a new form of life, a new frequency leading to a new form of existence. Knowing how to die is the key to our existence. This belief embeds itself within the New Testament, it being one of the clearest elements which are taught through the crucifixion of Christ. Christ brilliantly capturing that sinister Persian mode of execution and completely transforming it into a doorway of sorts, a doorway leading to a new mode of human evolution. No other world religion does that. None. Christianity is the clearest, cleanest doorway toward this evolution which I have found, and that is why I have stayed with it, regardless how much I am lured by the open road of Gnosticism or Buddhism or Hinduism. Christ unlocks the God-frequency within all humanity and points the way towards its activation. It's up to each of us to put this into motion.

Remembering death is remembering life. Remembering life is remembering death. Around and around. About and around the wheel turns, this way is the Way. It is the way of death and its acceptance within this lifetime which separates the wheat from the chaff. The members of the Esoteric Circle are the kernels of wheat gathered up by the master farmer to be planted after the apocalyptic fires subside.

## Surviving the Dry Season

What happens when the shots of dopamine or Jack or meth don't hit like they used to? What happens when you no longer 'feel' this goodness of God? What happens when you feel empty? This is the most common reason why people on the Way lose their way: they stop getting the 'goodies'.

On the night of January 9, 2005, during a small Praxis Research Institute retreat at 3 Barns in Devonshire, England Robin led a discussion about this dry season. He started out talking about knowing God, but this was a different 'knowing.' Robin referred to a knowing of God, but of God in a different form. He said everyone thinks they know God few know God well enough to talk about 'him.' The spoke of the 'work' guiding you *over* the gap between the two kinds of knowledge and if you start getting help from this first kind of knowledge then you will obtain help from another source. But first you must begin to get help from this first kind of knowledge, and this all starts with going inward, psychologically. We in the West fear this the most: the emptiness of the inward life. We fear this above all. This silence is like death itself. We move about, in search of any thought, any color, any feeling, anything to bring about the end of this silence. We are so heavily centered on our physical experience of this world that we use the motor center to guide us and direct in defining the legitimacy of our spiritual experiences. But we must learn to settle into this emptiness and wait, not being distracted by our expectations of what defines a true religious experience.

During this retreat I was right in the middle of a deep spiritual crisis. I was at *the* spiritual crossroads as I was still going through the aftermath of a painful divorce and trying to raise my 4-year-old son as a single Father. I was face to face with the reality that I knew nothing about the religion I was teaching and preaching about as a pastor. I was meditating intensely, most often during the middle of the night and I was waiting…I was waiting in that deep cavern of my psyche, waiting for the resurrection…waiting for sun as Jim Morrison said…Robin knew this and during this evening talk, on a cold and wintry evening there in Devonshire he said this, "You need to keep responding to God even when he stops bringing you the goodies…Peter, you understand what I'm talking about, o.k.?" He smiled at me and chuckled as he looked lovingly at me. I shook my head yes as we maintained eye contact with me for several seconds…it feels as though he is still looking into my eyes, radial energy pouring into my psyche, a love that is so uncommon here in this dark place… …he went onto speak about the need to look within where you will meet a 'greater emptiness' which increases in its subtlety the deeper you venture into this emptiness. You must go beyond what the ordinary psyche responds to and remain awake during this experience. You must acquire a strong momentum which requires a heart of fire, not a heart of flesh. He said specifically that this is not an evangelical experience, but a form of yoga. This darkness is evidence that you have entered the cavity within your psyche which is the actual 'heart' which Scripture refers to…if you can stay here in this place long enough then "the sun will rise, but it is a different sun."

If you are in this dry place, then you must stay here and accept that you are here…and wait upon the Lord…wait. Robin says explicitly that human beings are animals and all this work on our 'selves' is about changing this situation. You are an animal. Remember this. Dying in each moment of every passing day…shedding the old scales of karma in your own personal cave of Brahma each and every moment…dipping your soul into the ice bath of the grave, the cold, deep darkness of timelessness where space and time overlap and you realize you are the Temple, you need look no further…you are the Temple which you seek…and within that Temple/Cave, you will find the nothingness which you were seeking and it will be all you need, filling your soul with a lightless brightness, a whitish-yellow energy of love which encompasses the entire beauty of the Universe.

## What is the Point of This Work?

What is the point of this work?  Robin said we are trying to build a "coherent, integrated structure for the psyche and then deliver it to God.  This is what makes us human beings different from other animals.  The response to conscience is what drives the growth toward God.  We are born for a purpose: to attain Theosis…this is the Tradition's answer to the question of purpose within human existence.  This is not a fad.  This is not another passing popular method driven by social media like ice baths or frequency bathing on YouTube to decalcify the Pineal Gland and release DMT or micro-dosing psilocybin mushrooms all the while pretending that Terrence McKenna or Wim Hoff or Dr. Joe Dispenza are prophets of the New Age.

This *is* the Esoteric Path and…and it takes time. Theosis can't be 'achieved' through a simple readjustment of breathing patterns and frequency exposure. You can't 'hotwire' the Holy Spirit.' It takes time to awaken the human potential within you…this potential being the actual process of Deification of God within a human being. Spiritual awakening isn't just about an increase in dopamine. If it is then this spiritual awakening you are so eager to achieve is just about the search for another drug, masquerading as a spiritual journey.

The point of this work is about re-awakening the 'god' within you. There is no shortcut to this journey.

# Chapter Nine:
# Illumination

## Maurice Nicoll and being invisible

In Maurice Nicoll's book entitled 'Living Time,' he begins by talking about how any one of us is essentially invisible as we really can't catch a true glimpse of who we are as "all our thoughts, emotions, feelings, imaginations, reveries, dreams, fantasies, are *invisible*. All that belongs to our scheming, planning, secrets, ambitions, all our hopes, fears, doubts, perplexities, all of affectations, speculations, ponderings, vacuities, uncertainties, all our desires, longs, appetites, sensations, our likes, dislikes, aversions, attractions, loves and hates-all are themselves invisible- they constitute *'oneself'*…we do not understand *that life, before all other definitions of it, is a drama of the visible and invisible.*"
It is through this realization…an admission if you will…a confession of what you know is right and true that you begin (you've only just begun) to set your feet on this esoteric path towards a state of permanence. To know that you are real, you must admit that as you are now, you are invisible. You and who you think you are a fleeting, ridiculous blink of a cobalt black Raven's eyes, sitting in the Mulberry tree by the

river. You are nothing unless you develop permanence, a solid state of permanent spiritual matter which can (in various degrees) survive the death of this body. This survival after death is what this is all about. We toy with this idea of resurrection and think that we have attained it automatically by church membership or baptism or a declaration at the altar at age 11...but this is not so. We are invisible until we aren't invisible...this becoming visible is the resurrection which the ancients speak of, it is what St Paul speaks as the 'new man' allowing for the old man to fall off as a scale off a snake's skin falls into the spring leaves sitting underneath that same Raven blinking once again, an entire life-span in the blink of a Raven's eyes.

Illumination? Indeed, it comes when you realize you know nothing about illumination, and you mean that...you really mean you know nothing.

### The self-remembering and Franz Kafka

In the darkness of your invisibility, you can then begin to remember...self-remember to be more precise. What is this self-remembering? This is the grand question which beckons us on in the growing darkness: does anyone remember? It needs to be said, an obvious point really...but it's over. Our civilization and the mythology which was its foundation is over. The coming storms will break our circle that we have drawn, re-drawn and re-drawn for the past 900K years, and we will have to fend for ourselves in the darkness…unless we make sure to keep this circle unbroken. This is the key.

We within this Esoteric Circle are vessels of the living God, the truth that has threaded its way through out DNA from the beginning of the beginning. It is why those of us within this circle have felt so distant from the world in which we have been thrown into, as if tossed overboard into some dark sea at midnight. I have never felt at home here, never. Even my early childhood experiences with education were seen through the eyes of someone who was deeply and sincerely cautious of something nefarious which I had not seen or heard of felt, yet. Being born with this deep fear of the outside world, the world beyond my home, neatly protected by two amazing parents and a wonderfully comforting older sister, however…that outside world always lurked beyond that front door…taking the form of people and institutions and bureaucracies which not only were not interested in my well-being and progress, but taking it even further, wanted me silenced or extinguished. This is why the Gnostics rang so true for me and why Charles Ashanin's experience was so relevant to me. He too felt that the world we were thrust into was filled with evil influences which oftentimes inhabited human beings. It was this idea which attracted me to certain writers, particularly Kafka.

This is why the Czech Existentialist writer known as Franz Kafka was such a huge influence in my twenties. I have a wonderful Jungian analysis of Kafka written by Daryl Sharp entitled *'The Secret Raven: Conflict and Transformation in the life of Franz Kafka.'* Sharp quotes and shares doodling and sketches from Kafka's *Diaries* where Kafka shares his notion from an early age that he was alone, isolated, and fearful of this outside world. Kafka writes on October 17, 1921,

> I don't believe people exist whose inner plight
> resembles mine; still, it is possible for me to imagine
> such people-but that the secret raven forever flaps
> about their heads as it does about mine, even to
> imagine that is impossible.

In another entry Kafka writes, "I have seldom, very seldom crossed this borderland between loneliness and fellowship, I have been settled there longer than in loneliness itself. What a fine and bustling place Robinson Cruso's Island in comparison!" He saw this world as the Gnostics described: a prison. In a conversation with a young poet named Gustav Janouch, Kafka said, "I am now going home. But it only looks as if I were. I mount into a prison specially constructed for myself, which is all the harsher because it looks like a perfectly bourgeois home and-except for myself- no would recognize it as a prison. For that reason, every attempt to escape is useless. One cannot break one's chains when there are no chains to be seen."

Those of us within this circle, those of us who hear this deeper tune being played by an unseen choir humming behind the trees and rocks and babbling brooks…we hear such a different tune that it isolates us from the rest of the pack, setting us aside…causing us to experience this place as an Oubliette which we are trying to escape from (with the help of a guide). This is done to test us, purifiy us with this refiner's fire to see if each of us has developed some sense of permanence within our nous (our psyche). This idea of permanence is key as it is the equivalent idea to salvation. If you have not developed a degree of permanence, then a 'return' occurs. Mouravieff writes in chapter 14 of Gnosis 1;

> In the Tradition, we mean by victory over Death the victory of our perfected Personalities over Death. This is the meaning of Salvation, object of prayers and aim of the religious practices of Christianity…Death is an astral abortion. Salvation comes with the second Birth, when the entirely developed and born Personality is indissolubly joined to the real 'I' to form an *Individuality*. Once born, this *Individuality* no longer depends on the physical body, in the same way that the child who has been born does not die, even as his birth has been at the cost of his mother's life. (page 130)

According to the Esoteric Brotherhood, salvation is only possible for those who have crossed over a certain threshold of spiritual evolution. This is the process of awakening, purification, and illumination. It is the process of achieving this second birth while you are still here in your body influenced by these particular energies which inhabit this particular planet. When the mysterious labyrinth of your psyche (nous) can be explored and discovered and mapped like the lost Atlantis then you will achieve this second birth. This wonderful Oubliette-like planet of ours grants us all the energies we need to achieve this second birth. We must learn how to 'listen.'

Then you will be ready to return to your heavenly Father without any biographical or semantic baggage of this world, with having been drawn to Being, soul melting into Soul, heart loving with the tender whispers of Heart. All the while neither you nor your heavenly Father loses anything of your original nature, this co-mixture alchemically separating the two, drawing together but not blending into one. Your true Personality, after having been fully developed here within the Oubliette will return as a healthy cell to the body of the One and participate in the overall goal of the heavenly Father: a total transformation of all of Creation into an expression of pure love, the energy of the Ages which sustains all Life of the Cosmos. This is the goal of the Esoteric Circle.

The real question is: who will survive and how will it be done?

To put your spiritual awakening in perspective it is key to point out that the Earth, that little blue speck that we appear to be our intrepid space traveling cousins as they approach our solar system is one living, breathing organism. All living, organic life on this organism we call a temporary home is a part of the health of the entire system. In short, the main goal of our organic Earthly existence here is to become a healthy 'cell' in the body of this organism. Left to the forces which guide and direct life here (Mouravieff, speaking on behalf of the Esoteric Brotherhood terms this force the "General Law') we are born asleep, we live in sleep, and we die in sleep and when our bodies cease to generate breath we return it, having what Mouravieff calls an 'astral abortion.' This means without sufficient effort (even super efforts) at development of the higher levels or 'centers' (what St Paul calls the 'gifts' of the Spirit in I Corinthians 12:1- 31) you simply do not evolve, and you return, and the cycle begins again. According to this concept there is no universal salvation. To 'find' salvation you must evolve. This begs some questions, doesn't it?

### Mouravieff and the Doctrine of the Present

Mouravieff and his Gnosis Trilogy are key here as a key

to your illumination. Let's look at Mouravieff's thoughts on this subject toward the end of Gnosis 1 where in chapter 19 he writes,

> "...our concept of Future and Past is a relative concept, belonging to the limited intelligence of *exterior* man, when objectively, nothing exists except the *Present,* a *film* which-for any given cycle-contains all the Future and all the Past.
>
> We can now understand better this enigmatic and grammatically absurd phrase of Jesus that says '...*before Abraham was, I am.'*
>
> We can better understand that *esoteric work on oneself has the essential aim of broadening the individual slot that opens directly on the Present.*
>
> The uninterrupted succession of dP's [a term which stands for 'differential of the Present' which is the breadth of the slot with which one can observe the present] permits man to live on a line of Time. But the slot belonging to *exterior* man is not sufficient for him to perceive Future and the Past within the same broad *Present,* and so benefit from this permanent existence. In order to achieve this, the slot must be suitably enlarged.

The perception of the 'I', within a *Present* which embraces Future and Past, is none other than the consciousness of the real 'I'. The *Present* conceived in this way is *Life;* the slot three seconds wide is the famous *straight gate.*

'*Enter by the straight gate,*' said Jesus: '*for wide is the door and broad is the path that leads to perdition. Many are they that enter it. For straight is the door and narrow is the Path that leads to life, and few are they that find them.*' [*Matthew 7:14*]

And it has a lot to do with the concept of being born again which Jesus speaks of, but then he died on the cross, didn't he? Having contact with his Astral Body would be nice, right? But Christ says, 'let the dead bury the dead.' What does he mean by this? Does he mean breaking the bonds of all these ruts and grooves you have formed throughout your life on this Oubliette...not to mention the seemingly unbreakable bonds created by your Karmic burden...how do you stay in this moment in order to escape the bonds of the past and the present? How?! The key is to learn how to stay tuned to the moment!!!!In order to do that you must shed your inherited and personal past.

Let's revisit Mouravieff again as he immediately follows up on the above passage to end chapter 19 with this caveat about a prerequisite to widening this door...

It is useful to comment on the last text quoted, while examining factors which aid or hinder access to the *Way*. This completes and explains what has been said above. Talking with a rich young man, Jesus exclaimed, *Children, how hard is it for them that trust in riches to enter the kingdom of God."* [Mark 10: 24-25/Luke 18: 24-25] Then he added: *'It is easier for a camel to go through the eye of a needle than for a rich man to enter the kingdom of God.'* [Mt 19:23-24/ Mark 10:25/Luke 18:25] The question is: who is a rich man? Rich, in the esoteric sense, is someone who assigns real value to Personality, who places his confidence and hopes in it. This is independent of whether he has many belongings or possesses nothing…To set out on the *Way*, man must necessarily go through an inner collapse of the Personality, what we call *moral bankruptcy*. Then he will know the vain illusion of pride, and the true value of humility. Rich man or beggar, he will have become *poor in spirit*. Now he can easily slip through the *needle's eye*, for it is said: *'Happy are the poor in spirit, for theirs is the kingdom of heaven.'*

There is no other form of time except the present moment. The past and future are illusory and illusion, connected to nefarious places, like psychic portholes to spiritual programs which are designed to steal our present moment from us…until you get to this point where the present is your obsession, your only place of refuge, your one true home then these teachings are just theory. These teachings must penetrate your psyche, awakening, purifying and illuminating the dark nous and allow it to begin receiving the frequencies of the Higher Power of the Risen Lord into your mind, creating a new creature out of your old karma-driven, human frame and set you on the path of righteousness…all in the name of being a source of uncreated light for this world, allowing God to once again enter into this place and continue the transformation of the created place… Jon Gregerson's book entitled 'The Transfigured Cosmos' sat in Dr. Ashanin's library for years, somehow journeying onto my shelf.  The other day my attention was somehow directed toward this little volume of 4 essays on Orthodox Christianity and I was led to a story toward the back of the book.  I stumbled upon a story of two cave-dwelling monks who had both back-slidden one night with prostitutes.  One was despondent, horribly despondent and overcome by his bitterness while the other acted as if the night had never occurred and returned to a life of holiness, eventually being transformed in a *staretz* and holy man of high regard.  The other felt that he was irredeemable and abandoned his holy life and returned to his guilt, eventually condemned to death after robbing and killing a wealthy merchant.  Gregerson adds this quote from St. Isaac the Syrian when he is asked, "What is repentance?"  "Abandoning what has been."  That is the shedding of Karma.

…with each breath the attention is placed upon the seat or the eye of the soul, the place where St. Paul's 'helmet of salvation' sits protecting this antenna of the gods…the attention is placed here around the neck and head area of your body and you begin to be taught how to breath and wordlessly pray at the same time, with each breath and each thought simultaneously filling the chamber of your psyche with the correct frequency, therefore igniting the flame that has for so long been dormant, the layers of calcification begin to chip off (having been loosened by your consistent efforts and attention for all these years) and fall into the sewer of the descending lower centers and at long last removed from your system and out to sea…this angelic energy is now free to glow and flow and pulsate through the manger of your soul, magnifying the already present energy of the unknown God waiting present and filled with anticipation of your long sought after return to a condition of: listening.  Now, now you are able to listen to the Lord [the word 'Lord' literally meaning the 'keeper of the loaf'], the one who has the ability to created sustenance where there was no sustenance, the one who can create the uncreated with its very thought, having been at the source of your beginning and now sees you as a sane and healthy cell in the body of the Cosmos, needing this healing, needing you to be healed and now so joyous and glad within its own psyche that you have made the trip back to your source…you are the prodigal son or daughter who has now been spotted by the Father and the Karma Party is about to begin…

**Karma: the lost Christian Doctrine…**

The mystery of death and resurrection…every great religion speaks of it…some secret souls yearns for its memory to be unraveled, unfurled like a flag on a masthead…the Earth and all of its creatures speak of it in their constant dance with life and decay, pain and suffering, rebirth and reincarnation as the circle of life constantly spins and spins, creating opportunities at breaking the karmic burden which plagues each human life…

…have you ever wondered about Karma and whether it exists or not? Karma is traditionally thought of as a distinctive feature of Hinduism as well as Buddhism with the definition being an individual's mental and physical movements within time and space and the consequences of these actions. The reality of past lives and of reincarnation are an essential aspect of Karma with these actions and their subsequent consequences accumulating throughout the course of the constant return to this planet. Existence is essentially the work of moving beyond these past actions within time and space and overcoming the negative consequences accumulated within the lifetimes of these past lives.

The Doctrine of Karma has not been associated with Christian Doctrine but an authentically open-minded investigation into the cosmic nature of the origins of Christianity and its deep connections to the Mystery Religion and the Essenes reveals a deep belief in the reality of Karma within the first whispers of Christian thought. Within the investigation of this early thought comes sages like George Gurdjieff, PD Ouspensky, Boris Mouravieff, Dr. Charles Ashanin and Robin Amis…all giants within the field of Esoteric Christianity.

Let's start with Ouspensky who pre-Gurdjieff work 'Tertium Organum' still resonates as a seminal work with the Esoteric Brotherhood. In the chapter 13 he speaks briefly of the concept of Karma with a reference to a book by Mabel Collins entitled 'Light on the Path.' Within this short section he speaks of the illusion of time when he writes,

> …the idea of Karma, evolved in the remote antiquity of Hindu philosophy, is the idea of the unbroken sequence of phenomena. Each phenomena, however small, is a link in the endless and unbroken chain, stretching from the past into the future, passing from one sphere into another, now appearing in the guise of physical phenomena, now appearing in the phenomena of consciousness…If we examine the idea of Karma

from the standpoint of our theory of time and space of many dimensions, the interconnection of separate events will cease to appear to us miraculous and incomprehensible. Since events, even the most distant from one another in time are in contact with the fourth dimension, this means that they take place simultaneously, as cause and effect. And the walls dividing them are nothing more than an illusion which our weak mind is unable to overcome. Things are linked together not by time but by an inner connection, an inner relationship. And time cannot separate things which are inwardly close and follow one from another. Certain other properties of these things make them appear to us divided by the ocean of time. But we know that this ocean has no real existence, and we begin to understand how and why events of one millennium can have a direct influence on the events of another millennium.

The modern mystic Dr. Charles Ashanin speaks of this concept but utilizes a different term with a different connotation when he calls this 'pre-existence.' He says that we as homo sapiens have all pre-existed, in other words our cosmic origin is not this terrestrial planet but another realm and reality teeming with life. Dr. Ashanin says that our time here on Earth "is our time to re-think who we are and what we want and what our responsibilities are in this existence from God's mind."  Our job in this existence is to "remember the transcendent wisdom already given to us."  We are to say to God, "Lord, you have given me this space and I will make a sanctuary of this space," he says..."  There is something luminous about the physical world.  It is caught in the dance with the Divine."   Dr. Ashanin believes that the early church fathers knew about this doctrine of pre-existence with the belief that education as the process of awakening this knowledge already contained within each of us.  He believed we need spiritual technicians to teach us how to ignite this fuel or pre-existent knowledge within us...we need teachers of this knowledge...

Thus our time here on Earth is to be spent preparing for death, preparing for that moment when we will be judged for not only our actions in this lifetime but the accumulation of the past lives with a sense of repentance over any accumulation of negative actions and thoughts...Boris Mouravieff in his classic trilogy on the Esoteric Brotherhood entitled 'Gnosis' speaks of this hidden (not forgotten) doctrine of Karma.  He writes in chapter 14 of Gnosis volume 1, "...the principle of Karma, the Nemesis of the Greeks, the Archangel Uriel of the Christian celestial hierarchy-according to the Tradition one of the seven Spirits of God, who-alone in the Universe-never change.  He supervises the restoration of broken equilibrium at every degree of the cosmic scale."

He speaks of this burden of Karma within our existence and the act of overcoming this accumulation of this burden when he speaks of repentance. Mouravieff quotes from the Philokalia and St Issac the Syrian when he says, 'There is no unforgivable sin except sin without repentance.' Mouravieff writes, "Repentance is above all an act of consciousness, resulting naturally in benevolent and effective compensation for the error that has been made. This is the theory. In practice it is not so simple; it requires the minutest study of each case." In other words, an intense examination of our karmic burden and subsequent attention on this through the eros of repentance will 'clear the ledger' of this karmic burden and allow us to pass through to the next stage of our cosmic existence on the Ray of Creation. The eros of repentance is therefore one of the most important attitudes within our inner life as we use this time on Earth wisely, as a time of intense examination of not only the actions and thought of this life but of our past lives and our pre-existence.

## Karmic Decay

Karma and its burden is real and we Christians generally don't know of its existence…they don't understand this at all because they've not been taught it. This has tragic consequences on individuals as well as our entire faith. We have very few people within our faith who can teach this, pass it on and allow it to become a part of the vocabulary of spiritual journey and transformation.

The masses are asleep, asleep within their Karmic-burdened dreams...allowing other energies to lead them where they don't want to go but aren't awake enough to stop this somnambulism. As I've said before, organizations, institutions and entire countries can be subject to this Karmic Burden. Some would say entire planets can be subject to this somnambulism.

They/we/I am asleep in such a way as to be dangerously walking toward the cliff of Karmic decay, individually and collectively falling into the cycle they were born into and reassuring their destruction and definitive return to this cycle of woe and suffering and confusion which awaits an existence content to remaining in this unconscious state.

Mouravieff speaks of this Karmic decay in chapter 14, section 11, page 137 of Gnosis 1: Exoteric Cycle...

> Sometimes the disequilibrium between form and content can reach unmanageable proportions at a scale larger than that of States. It is undeniable that the crisis in which humanity is struggling since the beginning of this century contains the greatest dangers. Apart from

the direct cataclysm that the chain reaction of atomic explosion can provoke, there exists another danger of a totally different order, the accumulation of what we would call *karmic decay*. When such a case occurs, equilibrium is re-established either by a catastrophe such as the Flood or, if the weight of *Karma* is considerable, by intervention from the higher cosmoses. This was the underlying reason for the incarnation of Christ and His mission on earth, His torture and sacrifice. Quite obviously, the karmic danger which was accumulated just before His advent was real and great. The apostle John says that God sent His Son *'that the world should be saved by Him.'* We must believe that the preaching of Christ, followed by His sacrifice, counterbalancing the excess of karmic decay at that moment, re-established the equilibrium of the planet and so saved the world, and the whole humanity with it.

## What a time to be alive!!

…what a time to be alive in this world…with Artificial Intelligence and climate catastrophe nipping at our heals, where this awakening is now simulated and duplicated like it's as easy as a dopamine hit or melatonin or DMT or something deeper...to be alive in this world of ours...I mean did Jesus or Sidharta or Moses or Akhenaten have to deal with this type of world where A influences dart at us and there is absolutely NO escape from them?!! We are living in an unprecedented age which generations of our Earthly fathers and mothers never even imagined. Here we are being asked to leave the secure and dry shore of belief and acceptance and dogma and physical comfort, yet we never asked to be born in a time such as this. We never asked to be here, now...but here we are being asked to be the heroes...we are being asked to be the true heroes who have the courage to take on this darkness and embrace it...not only do we have our own inner darkness to confront and our Karma to escape from but we must venture into the cosmos and confront its literal darkness, all the while maintaining our humanity. Our core values of what it means to be a *homo sapien* will be stretched and torn and ripped apart. As the world quickly loses its moral compass those of us within this secret school must maintain our vision of truth and beauty, equality and compassion, freedom, and justice...

...our spiritual abilities are limitless, but we sit back and get caught up in our anxieties and miss out on all these messages from the other side and let them float into space, wasted bursts of precious notes to be heard by no one...

To be here on this planet at this time of such a transition is such a privilege! There is no time to be negative or frightened or combative or greedy or self-serving or fake. It is a time to be awake, taking in everything here as a gift, facing the headwinds with no hesitation. Nothing about it should be wasted. Nothing. Fear is dangerous. Why?

The fear which you feel is nothing more than precious, psychic energy hand-delivered to your enemy who wants nothing more than your complete apathy and surrender to the forces which have been nipping at you heals your entire life (and all your previous incarnations as well). Allowing fear to overtake you in this moment of planetary cosmic transition (PCT) is the last thing you should allow. It is literally fuel for your enemy. It is the very seeds for this crazy 'loosh farm' (as Robert Monroe would say) which we inhabit…this Oubliette which the Gnostics correctly labeled…it is the place which Jesus speaks when he describes the weeping and gnashing of teeth (Matthew 8:12, 13:24, 13:50, 22:13, 24:51 and 25:30…the other references from Psalms, Lamentations, Job and Acts all refer to persecution and NOT suffering)…this suspension within the outer darkness is quite literal I feel and should not be taken lightly. We have a binary decision here: go toward the light or be suspended within this darkness.

## The Crown of Thorns

The members of the Esoteric Circle need to claim this inclusion as a part of their identity as Children of the Light. We are not the conduits or worse yet the actual producers of fear. No fear should be willingly and consciously produced within the mind by an enlightened human being. This is imperative for the Esoteric Circle. Nor should any fear from some other entity be given haven within the mind of a human being reclaiming his or her glorious birthright.

The mind and the specific, physical area around our mind are the key to our salvation. In our collective 900,000-year history as a species it is why we have chosen a crown which fits nicely around as a 'king' or a 'queen.' The King or Queen's crown protects this area as a symbol of royalty, bathed in pink rose light from above, now descending below to sit upon this purified and rare mind which has evolved from a cloudy, feral existence to a deified, heavenly being. It is why Christ was so ironically bestowed with a crown of thorns to signify a new King, one whose flesh was transfigured with the quiet light of another realm, signifying a new way for us to follow. Indeed, it is this quiet symbol which we need to explore more as we journey on our path toward Theosis or Deification or…salvation.

It is this 'Theosis' (or glorification as Robin Amis calls it) which is our goal on this Esoteric journey. This is the hero's journey. If you've made it this far in this little book, then it most likely means you're already on this epic journey. It is a journey that is defined by irony: to be self-less you need to be selfish. You must take this journey so very seriously, as if your life depended upon it. If you have started this journey, then your literal salvation depends upon your completion of it. It begins with this inner magnetization and the formation of what the Mouravieff and the Tradition calls your 'magnetic center.' This magnetization does something within you that is so powerful that you are literally magnetized toward God, bringing understanding to reason and love to the heart and transforming your soul into Spirit, giving it a quality, the ancients call 'permanence' or salvation. This is the bond which connects all the religions no matter how old or how forgotten or how distorted from their original form. There can only be one Truth. Joseph Campbell was right: each religion is just a mask for the same eternal Truth. We are all worshipping the same God...

This God-consciousness rises peacefully above all doctrine and faith and theology. We within the Esoteric Circle do not have a theology...instead, we dance...in these quiet moments where the sphering stops within my past tense postmodern mind I hear this music and I dance and I realize that all the beauty of art which I have experienced all my life has been a vital accumulation of heavenly energy which I am using at this very moment to jump the chasm of my soul toward the Spirit I have always known was there. The art of the ages is the literal energy of God which is a vital spiritual fuel for each of us. Whether you are an artist or whether you feel a deep connection to certain types of art you must understand how important these experiences are for you. Art and music, science and religion have and always will be a vital part of your spiritual journey. Do not underestimate this. Do not underestimate the power of envisioning a civilized existence and a civilized society. Let us dream of a civilized world which will arise out of the ashes of this current rottenness that is Western Civilization. Let us dream while the world is in nightmare.

The artists and the musicians and the poets and authors and directors who have all helped me gather up the bits of gold on the beach…to these men and women I am in their debt…they helped me gather these heavenly influences, like manna in the desert all throughout my childhood and youth and young adult years. Without my awareness of their complexities these frequencies seeped into my nous and melted the hard eggshell of my heart and filled the chamber of my soul with the influence of the angels.

I see them all now, standing around me…Ouspensky and Gurdjieff, Kandinsky and Kurt Cobain, Charles Olsen and Sam Peckinpaw, Herman Melville and Kafka, Izzy Stradlin and Shostakovich, Donald Fagen and Walter Becker, Peter and Robert Buck,  Peter, Paul and the Mary Chain, the Minutemen and Men at Work in Dire Straits playing husker du next to the basement tapes with some Band and Bob Dylan Thomas going silent into that good night while Carl and Neil Jung play Old Maid with Sweet Jane as the stars of the night share the echoes of this blue sky as the exit music finally fades away and the R.E.M. sleep hits me hard and my eye lids flicker and fade and I realize it's only life after all…yea…

…echoing other human's words and feelings and insights…and I am left lonely…at some point this music needs to arise from the sanctuary of my heart…what about me? What about my words which come from my mind, which sink from the bottom of my coffee mug at my seat by my fireplace? What about me?  What about you? When?  When do the storms come roaring from the lion of my soul to say yes, yes here is what I've heard from the cave of my despondency, the black night of my soul, my soul…not St John of the Cross or that cross…what about my cross?  When will it be time to abandon my past and never return to my karmic vomit?  That is the rub…the constant aching question of sacrifice and death and bleeding and want and desire and abandonment and fear and the darkness into which we are all born and into which we all return…that dreaded return…we must all face the stark question: are we truly able to leave our collective and personal karmic past behind us, abandoning it forever and starting over? This is all about starting over and letting God re-write our personal story, unburdened by our father's father's Karma. But for the hero to advance and totally secure this abandonment, there must be a death, a cross to climb upon so we can rise above this physical world we've been born into, no choice of ours.

…but it is time, it is time for us to return to the darkness from which we came, to face that long dark hallway on our own and stop taking other human's words for it and experience this for ourselves…this long-avoided seeking after the light so that we can stop thinking about death and move past it toward the life that we truly seek…but before then we have chasms to jump over and ghosts to kill before we sleep…and ghosts to kill before we sleep.

## Lost in God's Consciousness?

When we reach this stage of Theosis do we just blend in with God, being slowly encompassed into the consciousness of something greater than we are as far as the evolutionary line is concerned? Are we just working toward allowing our 'being' to be absorbed into the greater consciousness of the more intelligent, more advanced being who created us? What is this higher consciousness that we are striving toward.

One of the key components of the teaching of Charles Ashanin was that as we continue to advance in our levels of consciousness our true Personality with all our talents and characteristics is allowed to shine brightest, so on the contrary we don't blend in with a higher being like some all-consuming Artificial Intelligence. Our individual Personality should be developed during our time on this Planet so that it is returned to the place of Origin, to the 'Father,' to the true 'Motherland,' to the place of milk and honey where the Prodigal Cell is exalted as an individual cell in the Cosmic body of God...it is here that we take the next step on the evolutionary ladder and truly participate in the creative process of the Universe where nothing is possessed. Nothing is defined. Nothing is obtained. Everything just is...we refuse to use force as a template for existence. We refuse to be animals anymore. We reclaim our heavenly birthright and stand upright as refined and renewed creatures of the Holy God who always lives within us all, now and forever more.

### The Age of Spiritual Decadence and Ultimate Hope

As a member of this ancient Esoteric Circle, you are

here because you have remembered your ancient past and taken your rightful place amid the others who are assembling here. Timelessness has been an ally to you as you have spent ages unpacking and discarding your physical (genetic) and psychic Karmic Burden. Unburdened by your toxic past…unburdened by your specie's violent and feral past you may now see (clearer and clearer with each moment of attention you are focusing on your head and your heart with positive emotions of thankfulness and gratitude in the name of the Risen Christ) what is occurring around you, what Nicholas Berdyaev called in his essay entitled 'The New Middle Ages,' "…a time of spiritual decadence, not of ascent."

What Berdyaev and Dostoevsky and Ashanin and Amis and Kafka and Melville and Camus and William Burroughs and Terrence McKenna and Nietzsche and Kierkegaard all saw was this: the rhythm of history changing and becoming catastrophic (Berdyaev, 'The New Middle Ages'). For the past century humanity has been quickly breaking ties with their inner life (Kafka in particular saw this in stories like 'Metamorphosis' and 'The Burrow' as well as Dostoevsky in 'Notes from Underground'), breaking ties with the soul.

### Where are my Allies?

The bureaucratic church has long ago lost its own

contact with this inner life and can no longer function as a true signpost. The 'church' should be pointing the direction toward the spiritual awakening which each of us is promised as our cosmic birthright. What I say here is to be taken quite literally and directly. Modern counseling and therapy make this realization and attempt to connect individual human beings with their inner life, but they have no method of re-connecting anyone with this Divine Element within the human mind and heart. Modern psychotherapy ultimately does not work because it does not have a methodical way of re-connecting us with the Esoteric tradition. It is just a band-aid on a deep wound, with no permanent healing. Drugs and alcohol can be literal portholes to other sinister dimensions, filled with darkness and isolation and ultimate destruction of this God-particle within the human mind and heart (the Logos).

It is so vitally important that you understand how easily you may lose your way…and never find this path again. Tread lightly into quick-fixes and short-cuts on this spiritual journey you are on. Once you have lost your way from this path then horrific, all- consuming A influences will begin to surround you and there will be no help from beyond which can reach you. You will be guided by voices which you think are there to help you but are there to fool you, stroke your ego, get you lost in nostalgia and memory and influence you so greatly that you will be literally lost without direction and without allies. You will be consumed, realizing to your horror that the opportunity at evolution has passed and you are lost, never to return to the path. This is where the 'weeping and gnashing of teeth' enter the picture. This is quite literal. For if you've heard of these secrets of the ages and then you turn your back then you are not fit for the Kingdom (and that's the Kingdom with a capital 'K'). You must awaken to this possibility before it is too late, working while it is daylight. You must earn a wage for the task that you have been assigned. This is quite literal.

You must search for a teacher of the Way and seek within you the quality which allows you to be teachable. There is a limit to what you can learn from study and reading about the Esoteric journey. This limit is the quality of your being. You must have character or what Plato would call 'Goodness.' It is well known that to try and teach the inner life to someone who is of low quality of character is considered a crime within the Esoteric Circle. In the early days of Christianity, the 3 years lead up to baptism was a crucial period of sorting out the low-quality human beings through the assignment of menial, grueling jobs. This would test the initiate to observe how he or she reacted to these degrading tasks. Would they react with resentment and anger, or would they react passive-aggressively just in order to gain admittance into the Circle or would they be teachable allowing for observation of themselves as they were tested time after time?

## The Stalls of Barchester Cathedral

A perfect example of this cosmic ingestion is the ghost story by M.R. James entitled 'The Stalls of Barchester Cathedral." Published in 1910, it perfectly explains the process of losing one's way and becoming surrounded by sinister influences which have two main directives: your isolation and destruction. Archdeacon Haynes let's his impatience and arrogance get the best of him (quite literally) as he hastens Archdeacon Pultney's exit from the pulpit of Barchester Cathedral, coming under the evil influences of the carved figures which adorn the stall or pulpit where he resides during each worship service. These carved figures originated from a tree (nicknamed the 'hanging Oak' by the locals) which had been used to execute local criminals a century and a half before, carry with them an energy which influenced those who were open to its dark calling. Haynes was carried down a dark path, from which there was no escape. This of course, is a ghost story. Ponder for yourself. Yet it is the same with us: we can reach a point where we begin to hear the weeping and gnashing of teeth, as Christ says. This is quite literal. Once we are down this certain path there is no more help from any entity.

We now live in a wonderful age, an age of promise and hope, yet it is an age of massive change and upheaval, barbarism and violence, forests burning and villages flooding simultaneously in a macabre dance of light and darkness. It is a time when truth is nearly impossible to comprehend as multiple voices of reason and relief are raised in desperation and anger and fear, all in the name of revival and renewal and a return to the good old days. But there is no shelter from this storm…. with one exception: you.

### I am all I need

Why do I say that you are all you need? Are we not comforted by cosmic community, family and friends, a key network of allies which we need to make this journey? Are we not in need of others to help protect us from this storm already upon us? Can we really do this on our own?

I say this because for you to truly attract these all-important allies, you need to collect your own energy in your own life, dealing with your own inherited and personal, organic Karmic burden. When you are toxic, you have a proclivity to attract toxic people in your life. Just think back upon these tough time in your life…were they not filled with toxic people who continued to 'pop' up on your path and surround you with negative energy? This negative energy shields you from the positive energy you need to move on and evolve.

You must work while it is daylight, building your own bridge to your inner world where a permanent 'outpost' or manger (if you will) can be built which will withstand the storm that is already upon us. You must work on your own inner life and bring peace to your own life before peace can be brought to this world. You literally stand on the frontlines of this epic struggle as our species works out our own collective salvation one *homo sapien* at a time. You. You matter to this cosmos.

This is a time of choice for you. It must be met with bravery (i.e. consistency of will) as you are willing to hold onto the Spirit of God as you _*feel*_ it yet letting go of your image of God as you __*know*__ it. This is an age where the emotional center *must* be developed. The motor center and the intellectual centers, we've got those figured out haven't we and look where that has led us, right? It has led us to a world where we are trapped within our physical bodies, the jail bars themselves are the five senses. We must develop the senses beyond our usual taste, feel, hear, sight and smell. We must seek the development of the emotional center…it is the development of the higher emotional center which is our goal within Esoteric Science. This is why the hero's journey is so key: you must be brave and let go of what you think you know about God and allow the Spirit of the Universal God to write a new book upon the pages of your heart…on the surface of your psyche, carving out new grooves and allowing a new language to be written within your sleepy psyche, the new womb of the Universal God.

And then a new manifestation of God can descend upon our hearts and the old wineskins can be thrown away and your nous can become the new wineskin and a new wine can be poured into you…your mind being a treasure trove of God's energy bestowed upon our species once again, ready for a new opportunity to allow God to speak through us in new and fantastic ways. Our species is ready for a new language of God to describe new emotions and new feelings where the power of our thoughts will drive our activities and relationships and desires. We will shrug off the old rules and dogma and broken theology and speak of new tasks and new species to meet as we venture out past the boundaries of our known solar system and into the cosmic territory of our galaxy, taking our place as co-creators of the Universal energy of a Universal God. Our days of being co-destroyers are over and it is up to those of us within the Esoteric Circle to hold onto this knowledge so we can make this collective leap into the next phase of our species' existence. We only need a few of us to take this dedicated leap into the future by diving deeply within our own psyche so that our species can be saved. Otherwise, we will sink into oblivion, the Anthropocene being a mere thin layer of radiated plastics and carbon-soaked garbage to attest to our presence here. We have within our psyches the ability to live on after our bodies decay. How many are willing to be the spiritual pioneers that are needed at this moment?

Not many are willing to do this.

This path is a lonely one, as you must turn your back on much of what is comforting to you to re-discover God *behind* the mask of Jesus Christ, or Buddha or Mohammed or Odin or Baal or Yahweh. As Robin Amis told me, 'There can only be one truth.' Amis perfectly echoes Joseph Campbell as there is the admission that amongst all these past, current, and future screams of religious conservative fundamentalism among all religions, there is truly only one God behind all these masks. Yet during our fateful hero's journey, we must follow one path, never deviating from this path. For me the path is Christianity, and my guide is Jeshua, Jesus Christ, the resurrected one who calls me back to my inherited place of light. But my God is not Christ. My God is the Light. Jesus Christ beckons me toward that light, inviting me toward the deification of my own soul as I work while it is daylight at returning my particle of God's mind back to God, fully developed and whole, harmonious existence with the Universe, at last. At last, the prodigal particle of Light has return to its home...let the party begin.

In the end, you must make these decisions as to which path you choose during this time of awakening during the Apocalypse. No one else can make it for you. There are no easy answers. You must be willing for new ideas to coming springing forth from your imagination, your Pineal Gland now broken free from your its calcified prison. You must use your own 'blood' to write your own words (as James Joyce remarked in 'Finnegan's Wake') in your own book, your own heart being that Holy Grail of legend filled with the literal blood of Christ intermingled with your own sacrifice. You seek comfort on this journey at your own peril. Seeking comfort and security and safety are a sign that you are losing your way when it comes to this hero's journey.

**Theosis is our Goal**

Theosis or Divinization is the goal of Esoteric Science. It is the underlying inspiration behind all the one true emotion: love. It is this love of our Creator and the desire to return to our true homeland which calls us back to the 'Father,' this cosmic reunion which Christ speaks of in the

Prodigal Son story in Luke 15: 11-32...under the haunting spell of language Luke is able to convey the image and the meaning behind Christ's message here in one concise and beautifully expressed glimpse of a true work of art (as Aquinas would say, containing wholeness, harmony and radiance to make it a true thing of beauty). In the Tradition we call this return to God: Theosis.

During a Praxis Research Institute four-day retreat on January 9, 2005, near the ancient cosmic energy source known as Stonehenge, Robin Amis spoke to the small group who had gathered in a drafty room around a calm and steady, crackling fire. (Robin's wife Lillian tended the fire with consistent care). Robin's presence was calm and steady, reflecting the fire in the nearby hearth at this homestead called Three Barns. I kept my notes from that talk, going over them time and again as they captured the energy like the photograph of a lightning strike. I could write a chapter on each sentence, but one short section has consistently stood out for me, and I want to share it with you here at this point in this book. Robin said, "Build a coherent and integrated structure for the psyche and then deliver it to God. This is what makes us human beings different from other animals. The response to conscience is what makes the growth toward God. We are born with a purpose: to attain Theosis...this is the Tradition's answer to the question of purpose."

This construction of a 'coherent and integrated structure' is our lifelong task, it is our 'salvation,' that mysterious concept which means little to our Western ears. But this is the practical application of that word, and it is the next evolutionary step for us as members of the Esoteric Circle.

And here is the kicker: for each one of us it is different. The goal (i.e. Theosis) is the same but the path varies. There is no one book or method of prayer or breathing or retreat or project which one can do or sign-up for and get handed a neat certificate. There is no ceremony of graduation or employee of the month hallway where your picture is posted or a pat-on-the-back gift card to Target or Wal-Mart. This is all about you and your own path. You will be guided along by your ever-present Guardian Angel who has been specifically assigned to you while you were still in your womb (Psalm 139). You will glide by certain books, certain music and live concerts, certain works of art and artists which resonate with you, and you are eternally attracted to, yet you have no Earthly understanding as to why you are so attracted to these artists and musicians. Above all you must survive. You will also meet strange, abrasive, and persuasive teachers in all shapes and sizes who look at you with the gaze of familiarity as you stand in the doorway of their classroom, lost and anxious on the first day of kindergarten or the last day of high school or a new elective in college. Above all you must survive. You will confront evil and narcissistic bosses who are attracted to you because you are an empath, and you will be given the choice to fight them or be consumed by them. No matter what, you must learn how to accept them for who they are in your life, evil and narcissistic and a rich blessing. Above all you must survive. You will fall in love with this man or this woman (like characters in a film), falling and getting up, falling, and getting and then falling again until you realize the rhythm behind each fall, and it captivates you. Above all you must survive clinging to the memory of your cosmic birthright. Children will be born holding collective Karma in your arms while you take in the unusually familiar fragrance of your infant's clean, soft head. You will die a thousand deaths as life hands you pain and suffering along this journey as you slowly…slowly realize what this is all about…taking each moment as a moment in and of itself and allowing the Spirit to guide you past your own Karmic burden of past pain and suffering to the doorway of your moment where you stand ready to be led past this threshold of the flesh and onto your long-awaited destiny: the return to your Maker, offering up a 'coherent and integrated structure' and then standing within this Esoteric Circle, taking your rightful place, that place reserved for you and you only. God is calling you back to your place within this Esoteric Circle. Above all you must survive and develop permanence within your sleepy soul, evolving into sweet Spirit.

## What are we collecting?

As far as the task of the members of the Esoteric Circle…what exactly are we collecting from the past wisdom of the ages?  We have been speaking of this new 'Ark' and how each of us are the new Noahs of our age but what 'animals' are we looking for to place within this new Ark?  Are we asked to gather up the greatest jewels of each of the major religions, plucking the gems and diamonds of Araby and place them in a plain wooden box and store it underneath some loose planks in the captain's cabin?  Then what?

We are quite literally gathering up the pieces of God which have been strewn about the world since the beginning of time.  Each civilization has its piece of the puzzle, trying to solve the riddle of why we a species can have such divine origins yet be so very fallen away from that image of its own Creator.  Diving courageously within our individual minds, stealing away from toxic past and the fears of the future, we settle the roots of our nous into this present moment and begin to be moved and transformed by the vibrations of the movement of our God.  With this courageous diving into our primal, individual subconscious we become a new thread helping to lead humanity out of the dangerous maze which is our existence. Only by relying on the collective energy of our past mothers and fathers of the Spirit do we have the wisdom to make it out of this maze alive. We must honor our past by relying on a purely human approach to this hero's journey, not relying on toxic technology to help guide our way through...we must remain true to our human approach.

This is not about putting together a quilt or patchwork of the common wisdom of all the ages. This is about diving courageously into our individual subconscious and allowing for the 'abandonment' of our past as St. Isaac of Syria would say. I would add that it isn't just our terrestrial past that we're abandoning but also our Karmic Past, that mysterious past from previous existence(s) which is carried with us like stowaways on a ship. We must abandon all this allowing for the individual and collective Karmic past to die and decay...then wait for a new dawn to arise within our individual soul. If enough of us have this resurrection, then maybe our species can experience a resurrection as well? Maybe we can arise in the glory of our divine origin with a new and relevant mythology for our present age, with a new mask for the God of our ancestors. There can only be one truth and this truth does not become irrelevant just because the environment is destroyed. The truth is the truth within us and around us, flowing like strings of energy weaving themselves through the quarks of our collective soul. This energy is the weaving of the thoughts of God within the fabric of our species and we need to claim this inheritance as the gold that it is. There is no need to search any further for it is all within each of us, if we only have the courage to take up this journey, this hero's journey. We need dreamers and artists and musicians and writers and shamans and mystics now more than ever. We need the reformation of the Esoteric Circle so that it will not be written in the grand book of Life that it was this generation which dropped the baton as the orchestra waited for direction from the maestro at the podium. It is our responsibility to make sure the music keeps playing but without a leader then the orchestra has no instruction about rhythm and tempo to keep the music flowing…our species needs this direction. We need these maestros, these artists, these writers, these shamans, these spiritual scientists (as Rudolph Steiner would say) to risk the hero's journey into the maze of the soul, gathering up a new message for a sleepy species ready to make the next step into the cosmos of the night.

### What Must I Do?

What must you do to take these next steps into the darkness of the soul? The answer is simple yet sinister in this simplicity: self-work. One must escape this re-occurrence which Mouravieff calls the 'Film' of our recurring life. We must escape this 'Groundhog's Day' scenario and achieve salvation in its true form when "true individual reincarnation becomes possible. This is not mechanical; it is done consciously, generally to accomplish a mission," writes Mouravieff toward the end of Gnosis I, (page 234). The Esoteric Orthodox (as opposed to the Exoteric Orthodox who know nothing of this inner life, only rumors) have a three-fold process of inward orientation:

1) Metanoia: going inward through meditation, with an attitude of intense humility as you realize this journey is toward the death of the physical body.

2) Hesychasm: creating silence within one's psyche where you can examine your 'selves' throughout each day, examining your pride, envy, anger, lusts, greed, gluttony and sloth-like depression and boredom.

3) Nepsis: being on guard to the attacks of the many spirits and entities which enter your body and psyche and take up residence there, feeding off your negative energies to keep themselves alive and awake in this Oubliette we cohabitate together.

There is a poem by one of the great Fathers of the early church named St. Gregory of Nazianzus entitled "The Problem of the Three Births of Man." Dr. Charles Ashanin wrote an amazing essay about this poem, and it is from this essay that I reference. St. Gregory speaks of three main relationships which we must: parents, God, and oneself. The first birth is from one's parents with this birth being psychological in nature. We must have *reconciliation* with our parents as people outside our past, present and future. We must objectify them to escape their grasp, admiring them without worshipping them. The second birth is the birth from God. This cannot begin by declaring that God is dead. On the contrary this about discovering and exploring your humanity in relationship with God. God wants to remain God, but God also wants you to be discover your true human existence. God gives you your human freedom for you to have a truly balanced relationship with God. When you are interdependent upon one another you discover that you are free from each other. This is the nature of true love. Lastly and most difficult of all is the birth of oneself. This is the greatest problem which we face as we enter the Esoteric Circle as you realize from the introspection and self-examination of the previous two births that your psychological existence is one of a fragmented legion, a mob. To add to the complexity, this life is not of your choosing with all the paradoxes and choices, the isolation and suffering. This third birth is dependent upon you seeing yourself NOT as the center of the Universe but as created by God. To find meaning in this crazy existence one must see existence through the eyes of our CREATOR. Meaning is seen only through our CREATOR.

These 3 births are psychological in nature and this point is very important because this inward, psychological birth releases our energy for true and vital, life-giving creativity. It is only *then* that we can truly, truly begin to be creative, co-creators with God so that we can allow God to live and create through us. This is the key. If you're wondering: what do I do now? I have an answer for you: learn how to meditate, begin to examine your inner life and begin to let go of your burdens, worries, daydreams, resentments and fears which you lead you around obsequiously by the nose. Discover your individual and collective Karmic past and learn how to observe what is you and what isn't you. You must learn how to listen psychologically. Praying is truly about one thing: listening. Praying and meditating aren't about talking to God and giving God your list of desires for money and things and relationships and jobs. It's much deeper than that. You must learn how to listen to God first and foremost so you must learn which thoughts are your thoughts and which thoughts are not your thoughts. Sort-out your mind…sort it out. You are being influenced by ghosts and demons and diablotins and you don't even know it!  How are you supposed to listen to God when you can't even listen to yourself?

Learn how to tap into your creative side and go for it. Create, create, create…then create some more…write, paint, sing, play music, dance, write poems, write your memoir you've been thinking about.  Artists will be our new shamans of a new age.  We need artists for they know how to listen beyond their Karmic burden.  The artists will be the saviors of our new age, they will lead on as they tap into their collective consciousness, bringing up diamonds from the mine of the soul, discovering vast new lands within the quark of the soul, realizing the long sought-after whisper of the strings of energy at the core of each electron that vibrate within our bodies.  It is this energy which we are trying to make us want to be reborn in a new image for a new time.  A new time dawns upon us…we must be ready.  We must prepare our psyche and return it to our Creator.  But make no mistake, we are entering the desert where the old ways will not be relevant to the task at hand, that being survival.  We will be tested beyond belief; each generation being tested like never before as the species and the planet descend into barbarism and a feral existence, we thought we weren't capable of…but we were wrong. There must be those amongst these rabbles who remain civilized, and this group we call the Esoteric Circle.

Let us recall what Boris Mouravieff writes about the Esoteric Circle toward the end of Gnosis I,

> It is important to clearly grasp the difference which exists between the *film,* a mixture of possibilities, and reincarnation in time, which belongs to the domain of the Real, and to understand the meaning of this difference. At the time of the second Birth by crossing the *second Threshold,* man escapes his bondage to the *film,* and enters the domain of redemption. He is then admitted into the Sacred Brotherhood of *living Beings,* called in the Tradition: *The Great Esoteric Brotherhood.* The Apostle Paul tells us: '*and we know that to them that love God, all things work together for good, to them that are called according to His purpose. For whom He foreknew, He also foreordained to be similar to the image of His Son, that he may be the first-born among many brethren.* [Romans *viii:28-29]*
>
> The *Great esoteric Brotherhood* is an unshakeable force: those who are part of it are no longer subject to illness and sorrow. Death loses its hold over them. On their own scale, following the example of the Lord, they too have *overcome the world. [John xvi: 33]*

### Forgive Me

I try and convey a simple truth in my little words for as

we all know it is not through words that we are saved, but through human relationship which is able to transform us as the Spirit moves through our sleep species with magnificent agility through the eyes…the truth that underneath all the guttural sounds which have been produced during my little life sometimes seeps through to the surface of my consciousness and onto a page or two. These brief glimpses of truth need to evolve into a permanent state of being, shedding the 'false self' and produce during this brief life span a permanent state of being so that after the separation of my soul from my earthly flesh there is something that remains in order to return to my Creator…this is Theosis…ahhh, but my words fail me…I cannot sculpt them, blend them, rediscover their rhythm in order to convey to you the meaning of the word 'love' so that you know *and* understand both at the same time, allowing this energy to penetrate into the secret chamber of your soul…to the place where the echoes of your Creator reverberate with a frequency which transforms your cells into something eternal, made to live on without the help of this frail, grass-like body…an illumined body of light, glowing with a light which does not burn out, but which simmers with a brilliance, as if it were a captured moment of dawn as the sun weaves its way through the April Maples, blending with the space in one eternal moment…it is within that moment that the Light is held, like the heart's long held silent spring gushing out into this newly created space that has miraculously sprung out of the tender shoots of light and energy and communion with the Creative energy, the Generative principle, the eye of the soul of the Universe itself, speaking to the child of Lux.

It is this space which we call Theosis. It is the returning to God what is God, the flesh shed away now like scales. The true being shining through with radiant light encompassing everything, healing all your past and securing your future by capturing the present. It is within this formula that the heart of Christianity lies. This is the resurrection: this rebirth within each moment of your Earthly existence. The accumulation of energy throughout this process of rebirth is the energy you need to acquire permanence or Theosis. Then the secrets whispered to the angels will reach you and you will have the ears with which to hear (Matthew 13:9).

Then…you can move on from this Oubliette…climb out and see the break of day. The sun rises for you child of Light. Your task is at hand. Reclaim your divine birthright.

# Epilogue:
## The Sound of Flowing Water

Now we begin a new walk, a walk through the village. Not a soul around. My dog Wanda leads the way. Fearless. Loyal. Alert. Her nose to the ground and always alert. Always alert.

It's the 6:59 a.m. light sun through the young leaves, touching our faces. Early May. Another awakening. There's still a chill in the air, a blending of seasons. Recent memories of deep frost and now the lurch toward Spring. Now it is here. Akhenaten's glorious and golden sun soaking into my soul as we walk down a path toward the water…toward the mesmerizing frequency of the flowing of water on an ancient stream bed. The smoothed handle of my walking stick in my left hand. The sound of the scraping gravel blends with the Cardinals singing above me. I use my stick and flick a large rock in front of me as we make our way down the path toward the Menomonee River. Rocks. We're all just rocks slowly making our way toward the river (it seems) everything is being drawn to the river. I too flow toward this river, like a drowsy pebble pulled by some force. It seems I have always been walking down this path that leads to this river. A long dark path it has been but now, now, the sun shines.

Along the path, Quaking Aspens and Boxelder, side by side there are invading Japanese Honeysuckle with native Black Walnut trees (everywhere Walnut trees) and then the Black and Red Mulberries, Dogwood and Redbuds filling the gaps.  All with their gnarled roots pulsating out of the damp soil, and muddy banks to the edge of the river where time ends as the gentle sound begins…the frequency of the now is here at the edge of this river and I have finally made it…here…now.  Such a long journey to get here.

The Menomonee River in Wisconsin…it's the only river I've ever known (evidently), and I, like some solipsistic shaman drawing me back to its humming edge have walked for five plus decades in my bubble of thought to this place and breathe, finally breathe this oxygen into my pink lungs.  My entire life being a journey back.  Here.  Listening.  Now.

Into this shallow forest I step, as if into Chartres Cathedral itself I step.  I hear the frequencies of life differently now.  This now where the light soaks through these agents of time to my time-worn face, I am addressed equally as a creature of the same creator, the same whisperer of calm truths flowing through the red lips of the energy I long to return.  That energy I call her by a crude name: God.  But she is much more than a name.  She is much more than a name.  She is a frequency behind the name.  A humming puzzle piece which fits and flows into that sanctuary space within my skull. My head is my sanctuary, a glorious crown of thorns I wear intermingled with 1,000 rose-colored pedals…all merging together as a frequency of Universal consciousness within the bell tower of my mind.

I walk on the path around the ancient Willow Tree while the temporal world around me fumbles and falls with low frequency sounds of diesel engines on the bridge 50 yards away, I focus my attention on my head and suddenly I hear nothing now. My attention is like a shield shutting out the world of low frequency garbage and waste. Shutting out the world at least for this moment. It is within this moment I find eternity and I feel nothing but the hum, the rhythm within my psyche of the clear voice which speaks above my senses, my five drowsy senses. Only the river resonating through my soul. This sound of the river activating some beacon which has calmly been waiting for this moment of awakening. This river, my home. Reflecting the condition of my soul…still and deep and everlasting…peaceful and powerful and pragmatic…flowing upon an ancient bed toward the ancient sea where memory of previous returns lead each drop back to the sea, the sea which never sleeps, always flowing and turning over and over like the day and the night. Inevitable. Consistent. Uncontrollable. God.

Now I hear. Now for that ancient frequency that unlocks the real human that has lay hidden in the cave of my soul. It is time. Now. Time to be born again. Now. Enough of the waiting around, expecting to turn into a saint. I'm ready now. I'm ready to be born again. Now. Here on the edge of this river.

What has drawn me to this little creek, flowing over a 600-million-year-old coral bed? What is this sound which captivates me so much? What ancient memories are awakened by this river? My entire life has been a constant scraping my chin on the bottom of the desert floor. No water in sight. Was it this? Was it this sound that I've been hearing all this time? The sound. Yes, it must be the sound of this river, this river which whispers to me. The sweet sound of life lapping up the emptiness, like a sun within the sea of black matter.

Yes. My soul is a sleepy, dim sun waiting to burn bright in the frigid darkness of space. A quiet whisper of God's voice I have been. But now ready to sing full throated frequencies flowing from the center of the Universe, humming in the quiet cavity of my skull…the sanctuary of my God within the crown of my mind…

Wanda suddenly stops on the trail, traces of rabbits and mice and chipmunks who have been foraging during the morning hours before any diesel sounds drown out the voice of my watery God. I walk past her and find our spot beside that enormous Willow. I set up the tripod and prepare the camera on my phone. I remove my cap. Rummage through my backpack and find my dog-eared copy of "In Search of the Miraculous" and open it to the spot I'm going to read. I adjust my morning jacket and clear my morning voice and turn on the camera and open my mouth, saying…

…smooth, flowing frequency of the sound. I let my voice flow, like the rhythm of the water around me. Her voice has a flowing rhythm of wordless grace and mercy and love. I try to mimic her. My God. Her sweet voice of flowing water on the bed of an ancient river. Ancient. Timeless. Slow. Calm. That ancient river that gently cuts through 600-million-year-old coral that used to thrive here in Wisconsin as a mysterious and shallow sea used to exist here, back, and forth, back and forth over the bed. Long before the Triassic and the Tyrannosaurus…long before our specie's whispered genetic jump across our feral existence as mere crawling creatures upon this 4.6 billion year old planet…and here we are…still trying to escape that feral shadow of night within the soul of our *homo sapien* skull…still trying to escape the violence and fear and chaos which has led us, ever so steadily and slowly to this little, lapping river flowing lazily toward Lake Michigan and beyond, to the horizon…to a new frequency which is covering our little planet with the whispering of our Creator God. And here I am, a child still trying to reclaim my divine birthright as I hear a familiar frequency hum in the sanctuary of my soul.  Can you hear it?

Printed in Great Britain
by Amazon

39629355R00129